# Love, Beauty,
# and Harmony in Sufism

ALSO BY NASROLLAH S. FATEMI:

*A History of Persian Literature* (1600–1880)
*Life of the Persian Poet Hafiz*
*Diplomatic History of Persia*
*Oil Diplomacy*
*Dollar Crisis*
*Problems of Balance of Payment and Trade* (Editor)
*Sufi Studies: East and West* (Contributor)
*Multinational Corporations*
*Sufism: Message of Brotherhood, Harmony, and Hope* (co-author)

# Love, Beauty, and Harmony in Sufism

Nasrollah S. Fatemi
Faramarz S. Fatemi
Fariborz S. Fatemi

South Brunswick and New York: A. S. Barnes and Company
London: Thomas Yoseloff Ltd

A. S. Barnes and Co., Inc.
Cranbury, New Jersey 08512


Thomas Yoseloff Ltd
Magdalen House
136–148 Tooley Street
London SE1 2TT, England


Library of Congress Cataloging in Publication Data

Fatemi, Nasrollah Saifpour, 1911–
    Love, beauty, and harmony in Sufism.

    Includes bibliographical references and index
    1. Sufism.  2.  Sufi poetry, Persian—History and criticism.
I.  Fatemi, Faramarz S., joint author.  II.  Fatemi, Fariborz S., joint
author.  III.  Title.
BP188.9.F36            297'.4            78-54329
ISBN 0-498-02248-X

To Shayesteh
the wife and the mother who has made our work easier, our
life fuller, and without whom none of our achievements would
have been possible

# Contents

# Acknowledgments

Our grateful thanks are due to: Dr. Peter Sammartino, Chancellor of Fairleigh Dickinson University, for his valuable suggestions; to Professor Emil Lengyel, for reading this book and making useful suggestions; to Dr. Ali Shayegan and Mr. Amini, for many discussions of Persian Sufi poets and for reading a part of the book; to Sandra Asdoorian, for typing and checking the sources and documents; and to our many Iranian friends, for their encouragement.

Equally sincere appreciation is due to the following authors and publishers whose works and words are quoted in this volume: Institute of Islamic Culture, Lahore, for passages from *The Metaphysics of Rumi* by Khalifa; State University Press of New York; *Sufi Essays* by H. Nasr; Edward Arnold, for passages from A. R. Burn's *Persia and The Greeks;* Anchor Books, for Moscate's *The Face of the Ancient Middle East;* University of Chicago, for A. T. Olmstead's *History of the Persian Empire;* John Murry, for the *Hymns of Zarathustra;* T. Fisher & Unwin, for E. G. Brown's *A Literary History of Persia,* vols. 1 and 2; Clarence Press, Oxford, for Aziz Ahmad's *Studies in Islamic Culture;* Philip Allen & Company, for Burton's translation of *Gulistan;* Cambridge University Press, for Reynold Nicholson's *Divan Shamsi Tabriz, Literary History of the Arabs, Eastern Poetry and Prose;* Duckworth & Company Ltd., for Le Gallienne's *Odes from the Divan of Hafiz;* Oxford University, for A. J. Arberry's *The Legacy of Persia;* Turkner & Company, for Whinfield's translation of *Gulshan Raz;* Octane Press, for Whinfield's translation of *The Masnavi of Rumi;* T. H. Foulis, for Costello's *The Rose Garden of Persia;* Gibb Memorial, London, for R. A. Nicholson's translation of *The Masnavi of Rumi;* Messrs. George Allen

& Unwin, for passages from the works and translations of A. J. Arberry and Reynold Nicholson, *Rumi Poet and Mystic,* and Badee uz Zaman's *Mulana Rumi;* International Headquarters of the Sufi Movement, Geneva, for passages from Inayat Khan's *Sufi Message;* Routledge and Kegan, for passages from Whinfield's translation of *Khayyam;* Luzac & Company, London, for Margaret Smith's translation of *The Sufi Path of Love;* Everyman's Library, for A. J. Arberry's *Persian Poems;* Asia Publishing House, for Azad's *Tar Juman Al Quoran.*

There are other older writers and translators to whom we are indebted, and we would like to express our most sincere gratitude and thanks.

Since there is no uniform transliteration of Persian and Arabic words, we have followed the Persian pronunciations, and in quotations we have used the style of the original authors.

---

# Special Thanks

Our special thanks are due to Farivar Saifpour Fatemi, Assistant Professor of History and Political Science in Bergen Community College and our associate researcher, for his constant interest and valuable assistance in research of some of the sources of this book and translations of several of the poems.

# Preface

This is the second volume of a trilogy attempting to describe the origin and some characteristics of Sufi ideas, philosophy, and pronouncements.

So far most of the writers on Sufi poetry have emphasized its mystical and Islamic connection. The other aspects concerning its universal impacts and its roots as a part of Persian legacy and culture have received little attention.

It will be no exaggeration to state that the intellectual and national unity of post-Islamic Iran owes its existence to a rich literature produced by men like Ferdousi, Sadi, Rumi, Hafiz, Khayyam, Attar, Senai, and many other poets and thinkers. These men re-created and restructed those aspects of Iranian culture which had been blacked out, obliterated, or savagely distorted under foreign invasion and domination. Unfortunately, in all discussions of Persian Sufi poets, seldom has this important contribution been mentioned. For some unexplainable reason, the noble heritage of Cyrus, the glorious teachings of Zoroaster, the legacy of the Achemenian and Sassanian empires and their impact on the post-Islamic culture of Iran have been ignored. In other words, the real world of pre-Islamic Iran that shaped the mind, the words, and ideas of these immortal and universal giants has been disregarded.

Fortunately, these poets knew the pre-Islamic world and presented it to us in a language that enchants the saints and entrances the sinners. This is what makes greatness in a poet: to know his world, to interpret it, and to change it for the better. They were not only master of words, but they knew the reality of

11

their world and its challenges. They championed the brotherhood of man and justice for all. They admonished kings and potentates for not following the path of truth and for betraying their trusts.

Sufi Persian poetry is the biography of humanity. It forms the grand line of demarcation between the human and animal kingdom. It has become an institution. It has been the graceful ornament of liberty, a thorn in the side of the oppressors, and sworn enemy of those who exercise tyranny over the mind of the people.

Goethe believed that the greatness of Hafiz's poetry indicates the greatness of Iranian civilization. It has descended from heaven upon earth to soften and charm human savagery and ills. It also attempts to render our existence harmonious. It is the music of the soul.

Kings have come and gone, generals and conquerors have appeared on the scene and have disappeared without leaving any positive impact on history. But Sufi poets whose work is the outcome of an effort to understand the age into which they were born are still the idols of the people. They are idolized because their life and work embody the human moral conscience at its most pure and most persuasive. Their concern for freedom of ideas, their hatred of cruelty, their fight against hypocrisy and religious persecution, their opposition to injustice and inequities were qualities that endeared them both to their contemporaries and to posterity. Sufi poets were both spokesmen and guides, yet without pomposity, posturing, or pretention.

Poets like Sadi, Hafiz, Rumi, Attar, Senai, and Nezami based their works on events that they witnessed. It was the subject of human suffering in their time. The story of the time of these poets has been the story of increasing cynicism, manifestation of religious and political crime, and moral decay.

Their poetry and their songs are a reaction to an atmosphere of oppression, cruelty, and intolerance. They constantly endeavored to draw attention to the acts and actors who had produced this intolerable situation. For the Sufi poets of Iran there was only one human community, elegantly expressed by Sadi of Shiraz:

> All Adam's sons are limbs of one another;
> Each of the self-same substance as his brothers,

So, while one member suffers ache and grief,
The other member cannot win relief.
Thou, who are heedless of the brother's pain,
It is not right at all to name thee man.

It should be clear from this summary that Sufi poetry is something more than emotional and mystical religious utterances. It
is a reflection of the intellectual and humanistic culture of Iran.
It is the product of a fluent mind with great capacity for intellectual liberty and a profound dedication to integrity, truth, and
humanity. Its loyalty is only to absolute truth and individual
freedom. That is why the political and religious history of Iran
is so full of dissension and discord. That is why there is a per-
manent "stars war" in the intellectual firmament of Iran. Hafiz,
addressing his contemporary religious vigilantes, states:

Preacher, it is all in vain you preach to me,
Nor business of anyone's but mine
Where I have sinned and what my end will be.

Ferdousi claims that his poems defy fortune and outlive the
world's calamities. They are beyond the reach of thief, moth, or
rust. They are beyond the reach of the wind, rain, earthquake,
storm, and hurricane. As they cannot be stolen, expropriated, in-
herited, so they cannot be destroyed or alienated. They are an
eternal edifice surviving all the conquerors, kings, and kingdoms.

Persian poetry is an interpretation of both moral profundity
and national characteristics. In the works of Rumi we find the
wisdom, compassion, and spiritual values; in Sadi's work there
is statemanship, freshness of youthful feeling, wisdom, and reverence of old age; in Nezami's work, tenderness and loveliness of
nature; and in Hafiz's verses one finds love, beauty, frankness,
and intellectual freedom.

Sufi ideas and poetry are immortal and have immortalized
Iran. They are a comfort to the broken heart and a consolence to
the worried mind.

The great poets of Persia, according to Reynold Nicholson,
with few exceptions, have borrowed ideas and speak the universal
language of Sufism. They fall into two groups. Some are like

Hafiz, "by tantalising the reader, by keeping him, as it were sus-pended between matter and spirit, they pique his ingenuity and double his pleasure. Nearly every line is a play of wit." Love, wine, beauty, lover and beloved, are painted in the warmest and the most alluring colors. Others base their poetry on a loftier ethical system, which recognizes purity of heart, charity, universal brotherhood, compassion, harmony, and self-renunciation. "At-tached to this," continues Nicholson, "we find a pantheistic theory of the emananation of all things from God, and their ultimate reunion with Him."

Although, concludes Nicholson, on the surface Sufis favor Is-lam, they assert that all religions and revelations are divine and they are only the rays of a single eternal sun. All prophets have only delivered in different tongues the same principles of eternal goodness and eternal truth that flow from the divine soul of the world. The poems of this group are based on a transcendental pantheism. Virtue, as they understand it, is not an end, but a means. The end is union with God through love. If a country's lit-erature is rightly reckoned among its noblest heirlooms, the debt that Persia owes to the Sufi poets is beyond calculation.

Sufism and its literature, therefore, are children of the soil of Iran, "called into being by the deeper and truer religious spirit which the dry monotheism had stifled." Its source, apart from Islam, is found in Zoroastrianism, Buddhism, Christianity, and Greek philosophy. It has borrowed something from all of them, yet it is not identified with any of them. In the words of Rumi:

> What is to be done, O Moslems? for I do not recognise
>   myself.
> I am neither Christian, nor Jew, nor Zoroastrian, nor
>   Moslem.
> I am not of the East nor of the West, nor of the land
>   nor of the sea.[1]

Persian poetry, according to Sadi, revives the relish of simple pleasure in the hearts of rich and poor. It refines our mind and

---

[1] Rumi, *The Divan of Shamsi Tabriz*, translated by Reynold A. Nicholson; (Cam-bridge: Cambridge University Press, 1898), pp. XXVII–XXX.

inspires our heart with love and joy. It is interpretive both by having natural magic in it and by having moral profundity.

As with the first volume, the purpose of this book is not to write the historic development of the Sufi movement or to explain the activities of the different sects, cults, and orders or their rites and rituals, but to introduce American readers to some aspects of Sufi ideas and thoughts, their roots, and their impact on human society.

Furthermore, our hope is that in these days of political feuds, religious and racial conflicts, and ideological discords, this study may help us to appreciate the beauties of other cultures and help to build a world free of religious, racial, and ideological feuding and hatred.

# *Love, Beauty, and Harmony in Sufism*

# 1

## Sufis and Persian Poetry

Lo, for I to myself am unknown, now in God's name what must
    I do?
I adore not the cross nor the crescent, I am not a Zoroastrian or
    a Jew
East nor West, land nor sea is my home, I have kin nor with
    angel nor gnome,
Not in this world nor that world I dwell, not in paradise neither
    in hell;
Not from Eden nor paradise I fell, not from Adam my lineage
    I drew
In a place beyond uttermost place, in a tract without shadow of
    trace,
Soul and body transcending I live in the soul of my loved one
    anew!

Rumi

One of the richest and most melodic languages of the world is
Persian, so singularly adapted to the purpose of poetry that
there are acknowledged to have been more poets produced by
Persia than by any other nation in the world. There is in no other
poetry such variety of style or of content. Sir William Jones,
the eminent authority on Persian poetry, has justly claimed that
"the Persian verse is rich in forcible expressions, in bold meta-
phors, in sentiments full of fire, and in descriptions animated with
the most lively colouring."

Sir Gore Ouseley observes that "the mine of Persian literature contains every substance, from the dazzling diamond to the
useful granite, and its materials may be employed with equal
access to build castles in the air or upon the earth."

Persian Sufi poetry and prose are one of the strongholds of
the human heart and mind. For more than twenty-five centuries,
Persian culture has represented a struggle between good and
evil, between light and darkness, with the assurance that light
and goodness will destroy evil and darkness and eventually justice will replace tyranny.

The Persian poets and writers, with their passion for virtue,
goodness, and justice, led intellectual rebellion and dissent
throughout the realm and as a result faced prison and persecution with courage and love. They spoke loving words and declared
that a mind stirred by love can change confrontation into cooperation, hatred into love. These poets have painted visions of
heaven on earth through love, and each in his own way has produced his own description of a world devoid of anger, avarice,
hate, feud, and fight.

However, the secret treasure of Iran has seldom been presented to non-Persian-speaking people. Even today when that
nation has become well known because of oil and industrializa-
tion, its lyrical gems are unknown to most Americans. In this
second volume of Sufi studies a new collection of the work of
Sufi poets and mentors is presented with the hope that English-
speaking readers will find delight in these long-slighted treasures.

Sufi poets and thinkers have been and still are held in the
greatest reverence in Iran and the rest of the Middle East. Some
years ago a notable periodical, *Ayendeh*, asked a question: Who
were the greatest men of Iran? Many readers chose not kings,
generals, theologians, or statesmen, but poets, thinkers, philosophers, and pundits such as Zoroaster, Ferdousi, Sadi, Rumi, Hafiz,
and Al Ghazali.

If, as according to Voltaire, true greatness consists in having
received from heaven the advantage of a superior genius, with
the talent of applying it for the interest of the possessor and of
mankind, then men like Firdusi, Sadi, Rumi, and Hafiz are surely
greater than any king or statesman:

Conquerors, which no age has ever been without, are commonly but so many illustrious villains. It is the man who sways our minds by the prevalence of reason and the native force of truth, not they who reduce mankind to a state of slavery by brute force and downright violence, the man who by the vigor of his mind is able to penetrate into the hidden secrets of nature; and whose capacious soul can contain the vast frame of the universe, not those who lay nature to waste, and desolate the face of the earth, that claims our reverence and admiration.[1]

Political history in general is a collection of crimes, follies, and misfortunes, among which we have now and then met with a few virtues contributed by men like Cyrus. These are oases in a barren desert. In the times of darkness, cruelty, and ignorance that followed Iran's invasion by the Arabs and Mongols, very few political leaders appeared. None deserved the mantle of greatness as philosophers, writers, and poets such as Al-Ghazali, Ferdousi, Sadi, Hafiz, Rumi, Nezami, Khayyam, Attar, Senai, and Jami. They were the voices who sang the praises of honesty, dignity, compassion, and integrity and chastised the wickedness of the tyrants and oppressors. If mankind enjoys any human decency and rights, it is to these thinkers and poets that we are chiefly indebted for the happy changes. They were the courageous souls who exposed the villainous acts of kings and generals, the hypocrisy of theologians, and the brutality of the exploiters of workers and peasants.

[1] Voltaire, *English Letters.*

# 2

# The Rise of the Sufis and Their Doctrines

From farthest East to threshold of the West
I in this age am guide to God's straight road.
How can the gnostic pilgrims me behold
Beyond the Far beyond 's my soul's abode.

Ruzbihan

The keynote of Sufism is disinterested, selfless devotion, in a word, love.

Arabi

The first century of the Abbasid Caliphs was marked by a great intellectual agitation. Many new ideas were introduced by the Persians, who at this time were the dominant power in Baghdad. This was the beginning of the Golden Age of Islam. The first university in which studies of philosophy, theology, law, medicine, astronomy, mathematics, and natural sciences attained their importance was established in Baghdad, and non-Muslim translators and professors started teaching and translating Greek, Persian and Indian works into Arabic at the "House of Learning."

These new opportunities for learning, disputation, and discussion produced new religious and ideological theories such as rationalism, free thought, scholastic theology, and the Sufi mysticism.[1]

---

[1] R. D. Nicholson, *A Literary History of Arabs* (London: T. Fisher Unwin, 1907).

22

Most of these intellectual dissidents came from the eastern part of Iran and Iraq. It was in Khorasan and Basra, the intellectual capital of Islam, that a small group started a movement that maintained the principle that thought must be free in the search for truth. This group is known as the Mutazilites (Schismatics). In its earliest form, the Mutazilites were connected with the doctrine of free will and predestination. The Koran, referring to this question, is ambiguous. On one hand it says "Every soul is in pledge for what it has wrought";[2] "whoso does good benefits himself, and whoso does evil does it against himself."[3] On the other hand the Koran declares that "God leads men aright or astray as He pleases; that the hearts of the wicked are sealed and their ears made deaf to the truth; and that they are certainly doomed to perdition."

For the first two centuries the dogma of predestination was dominant. But about A.D. 780 Wasil Ibn-Ata, founder of the Mutazilites, declared that man is born with free will and responsible for his action. Furthermore, he denied the existence of the divine attributes of God on the ground that such attributes would destroy the unity of God.

---

Soon after Wasil's death, his successors started to propagate their rationalist views openly and candidly. The argument that shocked the orthodox Muslim community was the question "Is the Koran created or uncreated?" "Is it the work of God or the word of God?" The Orthodox belief was that the Koran existed with God from all eternity. Its present form was merely a transcript of the heavenly archetype. The Mutazilites, on the contrary, asserted their intellectual freedom. It was possible, they said, to know God and distinguish good from evil without any revelation. They denied the deification of the Koran but admitted that it was the word of God revealed to his prophet. Some free thinkers even started to criticize the style of the Koran, declaring that it could be surpassed in eloquence by the art of man.[4] For almost

---

[2] Koran 24:41.
[3] Koran 12:46.
[4] Nicholson, *Literary History of Arabs*, p. 369.

a century Mutazilite doctrines were burning questions in the Islamic world until Caliph Mutawakkil suppressed them in 847.

After the suppression of the Mutazilites the weapons of logic and dialectic were turned against intellectuals and free thinkers. A period of reaction and oppression was founded on the ruins of reason and rationalism. However, the ideal restlessness created by the Mutazilites and the political uprisings in Persia gave rise to other movements such as Ikhwan Ul-Safa and the Sufis, who endeavored to enlighten and humanize the reactionary world.

The origin of the word *Sufi* is explained in different ways. Some claim that it comes from the Arabic word *Safa* (purity), others connect it with the word *Suf* (wool). The former is accepted by many ancient Sufis, and Junaid of Baghdad, one of the most celebrated Sufi mentors, who died in A.D. 910, states: "Sufi is the one who has been chosen for his purity. Whoever is thus chosen and made pure from all except God is the true Sufi." Faridu din Attar (d. A.D. 1230), the famous Persian Sufi poet, in his book *The Memoirs of the Saints*, mentions both definitions, but he favors the word *Safa* (purity) over the word *Suf* (wool). Another famous writer and philosopher, Ibn Khaldun (A.D. 1406), referring to Sufis, states:

The way of the Sufis was regarded by the ancient Muslims and their illustrious men . . . as the way of truth and salvation. To be assiduous in piety, to give up all else for God's sake, to turn away from worldly goods and vanities, to renounce pleasure, wealth and power, which are the general objects of human ambition, to abandon society and to lead in seclusion a life devoted solely to the service of God—these were the fundamental principles of Sufism which prevailed among the companions and the Muslims of old time. When, however, in the second generation and afterwards worldly tastes became widely spread, and men no longer shrank from such contamination, those who made piety their aim were distinguished by the title of Sufis or Mutasawwifa (aspirants to Sufism).[5]

---

[5] Ibn Khadoun, Muquaddameh, quoted by A. R. Nicholson and translated by DeSlane.

Reynold Nicholson, whose research and studies of Sufism are still the best available, contends: "The word [Sufism] had a lofty significance which commended it to the elect. Nevertheless it can be tracked to a quite humble source. Woolen garments were frequently worn by men of ascetic life in early times of Islam in order that they might distinguish them from those who affected a more luxurious fashion of dress. Hence the name Sufi which denotes in the first instance an ascetic clad in wool."[6]

Regardless of the origin of the words *Sufi* and *Sufism*, the idea has had a great impact on the religion, the literature, and the role of life not only in Iran but throughout the Muslim world and beyond. Sufis were hermits, but they were also something more. They were the intellectual dissidents, the conscience of society, and the leaders in universal ideas and human values. "They brought out the spiritual and mystical elements in Islam, or brought it in, if they did not find it there already. The keynote of Sufism is disinterested, selfless devotion, in a word, love."

Little is known about the earliest ascetic tendencies of Sufis, but as time progressed, Sufis, like other groups, developed a negative attitude toward the corruption, cruelty, oppression, and suppression of the Omayyad and Abasside caliphs. They equated the perversive society and its government with evil. They lamented the fact that the Islamic Empire, stretching from Spain to India, had become as corrupt as the Roman and Sassanian empires that preceded it.

Hassan Basri (d. 728), the patriarch of the Sufis, sensed the danger inherent in a society that was interested in pomp, luxury, wealth, and conquest. Fear of God and punishment on the day of judgment seized Hassan so strongly that, in the words of his biographer, "it seemed as though Hellfire had been created for him alone." According to Louis Massignon, we find in Hassan "a realistic critical tendency" as opposed to the more "idealistic tradition" that prevailed in Kufa.

The orthodox Muslim represented God as a stern, unapproachable despot, requiring utter submission to his will. The Sufis, heirs to the intellectual and humanistic legacy of Persia, Arabia,

---

[6] See Nasrollah S. Fatemi, Faramarz S. Fatemi, and Fariborz S. Fatemi, *Sufism: Message of Brotherhood, Harmony, and Hope* (South Brunswick and New York: A. S. Barnes and Co., Inc., 1976).

India, and Greece and who later borrowed from Judaism and
Christianity, became true protestors against the conscienceless,
heartless society. They also condemned the slavery and hypocrisy
of the time. Rabia (d. A.D. 801), one of the founders of Sufism,
was a slave girl, set free by her master. She introduced elements
of selfless love into the austere teachings of the early ascetics and
gave Sufism the hue of true mysticism. Rabia's idea of "love for
love's sake" has become the central topic of Sufism.[7]

One of the many privileges that an observant mind enjoys
in this complex age is the fact that people today are as much in
need of ideals and spiritual leaders as at the time of Al-Ghazali,
Rumi, Junaid, Rabia, and Hallaj. Anxiety, instability, and desire
for peace of mind are as true today as they were in the ancient
Middle East or in England when Francis Bacon hoped that the
advancement of learning might save the world from its maladies.
Since the time of Rumi and Bacon there have been many physical
and scientific triumphs far beyond the human imagination of
their times. Scientific advancement has brought the face of the
earth nearer to the will of man. Only man, his conduct, and his
character seem to have changed very little from when Rumi
declared:

My heart is weary of these weak-spirited companions;
I desire companion of the Lion of God[8]
    and Rustam, son of Zal.[9]
Of this folks I am full of complaint, weeping and weary; I desire
the drunkards' screams and their lamentations. My soul is grown
weary of Pharoah and his tyranny; I desire the light on the face
of Moses, son of Imran.
Yesterday, the master with a lantern
    was roaming about the city,
Crying "I am tired of devil and beast, I desire a man,"
My state has passed even beyond all yearning and
    desire;

---

[7] See Fatemi et al., *Sufism*, in which is presented a historical evolution of Sufism
and the reference to saints and the mentors who contributed to the development
of Sufi ideas—Ibrahim Adham, Bayazed of Bustam, Zul Nun, Hallaj, Runi Hafiz,
Sadi, Alghazali, Nizami, Khayyam.

[8] Lion of God is the title of Ali, the son-in-law of Muhammad, and the fourth caliph.

[9] Rustam is the hero of ancient Persia.

I desire to go from being and place towards the
    Essentials.
He is hidden from our eyes, and all objects are
    from Him;
I desire that hidden one whose work are manifest.
They said "He is not to be found, we have sought
    Him long!"
A thing which is not to be found—that is my
    desire.[10]

Modern man is on the shore of a vast and dangerous ocean, still tumultuous, still very dark, still threatening to destroy him either with nuclear weapons or through terrorism, riots, and revolution. He does not know its lanes and distances, nor what safe and happy isles may lie beyond. "The ideal man [Sufi Attar] traversed the seven cities of love, but we have not yet crossed the turning point of a single lane."[11] The new inventions and technology, without the guidance of men and women dedicated to the cause of humanity, will venture forth, moving about with error, hatred, and anger, and eventually resulting in a total world destruction.

The question of man's personality, survival, purpose, and his goal is one of the most difficult problems in the Sufi metaphysics. Every Sufi teacher, poet, and savant asks: "What are we, after all? Apes? Or gods? Yazdan or Ahriman? Or Ahriman on the way to being gods? What is 'human nature' that appears to determine the destiny of man with so many tragedies? What are the foundations and elements of character and personality? Is human nature unchangeable or can it be changed? The same Sufi teachers believed that man can lift himself by his own bootstraps out of the chaos. At this stage he will be guided by God: "Thy existence is part of the existence of your Creator. If you are ready he will transform you in the same way that base metal is transformed through alchemy."

The Sufis believed that man's character is composed of different elements: cheerfulness, gloom, passion, and cold-hearted-

---

10 Rumi, Diwan Shams i Tabrizi, translated by R. Nicholson.
11 Rumi, Masnavi, p. 166, published in Teheran, 1924. Attar is the great Sufi mentor. (A.D. 1230.)

ness. Therefore, first he must understand himself and then control his inner purpose by submission to God and devotion to service. "To know thyself is to know thy God." This will be equivalent to being born again: "When man is born the second time, he walks over all causation; he rises above belief in the first cause and bears no grudge against the final cause."[12]

Shabastari, referring to this state of human change, declares:

That man attains to the secret of unity
Who is not detained at the stages on the road.
But the knower is he that knows Very Being,
He that witnesses Absolute Being,
And being such as his own he gambles clean away.
Your being is naught but thorns and weeds,
Cast it all clean away from you.
Go sweep out the chamber of your heart,
Make it ready to be the dwelling-place of the beloved.
When you depart out, He will enter in,
In you, void of yourself, will he display his beauty.
The ideal man is loved for his pious works,
He finds an abode in a "laudable station"
He finds a portion of what eye hath not seen, nor ear heard.
Until you cast away obstacles from before you,
The light enters not the chamber of your heart.
As there are four obstacles in this world,
So also the modes of purification from them are four:
First purification from filthiness of the flesh;
Second, from sin and evil whispers of the temper;
The third is the purification from bad habits,
Which make men as beasts of the field;
The fourth is the purification of secret,
For at this point the pilgrim's journeyings cease.
Whoso is cleansed with these purifications,
Verily he is fit to commune with God.[13]

The development of civilized man, said Eckerman, "seems to be a matter of a thousand years." "Who knows," replied Goethe, "perhaps of millions, but let humanity last as long as it will,

---

[12] Rumi, Masnavi, v. 3576.
[13] Shabastari, *Galshani Raz*. Translated by E. H. Whinfield (London: Trubner and Co., 1880), pp. 14–15.

there will always be hindrances in its way, and all kinds of distress, to make it develop its potentialities. Men have become cleverer and more intelligent, but not better, nor happier, nor more effective in action. I see the time coming when God will take no pleasure in the race, and must again proceed to a rejuvenated creation." This rejuvenation is what the Sufis are after and call it "born again" as an ideal man. The Sufis disagree with both Goethe and Nietzsche, when they state that mankind does not progress. The Sufis were the first to make distinction between physical and moral progress, between increase in physical power and improvement in moral purposes. They warn us not to confuse worldly comfort and pleasure with spiritual happiness. At the height of the power and physical progress of the Islamic Empire in Baghdad, Sufi writers told leaders that the enlightened Muslim world was unhappy because progress was a fever and race for power and wealth. Then they asked, progress for what? They lamented that a limited number of men had achieved enormous power to exploit other people, but of what use were these unprecedented powers and wealth if they had merely multiplied the ability of man to realize purposes so contradictory, so stupid, so cruel, and so detrimental to the welfare of mankind.

Man was born lord of creation, but his vile actions have made him master of suffering. In the words of Rumi, it is not power or wealth that makes you lord and master, but wisdom, service, and decency.

Happy is the man who was freed from power, wealth, and himself and united with the existence of a living purpose. The spirits that are liberated from their cages of greed are the prophets and saints (the ideal man). The man who is like a bird, a prisoner in a cage of power and wealth, and is not seeking to escape is either a fool or an animal. Worldly wealth and reputation are a strong chain. How is this less than a chain of iron?

---

The Persian Sufi poets belong to that group of noble persons who inspired people with their ideas of truth, contentment, universalism, brotherhood, and liberty. Like Christ, the Sufis believed that liberty is the ability to restrain desire and live free from the shackles of greed, prejudice, and hate. It is in this state, according to the Sufis, that man sees his God face to face. This is the vision of joy, satisfaction, and freedom. This vision inspires us to make peace with ourselves, our creator, and our fellow man. It is man alone who must bring felicity to his surroundings and alleviate mankind's suffering.

The Sufis lament the fact that man, who, according to the Koran, is the greatest creature of God, has caused more conflict and misery than any savage beast. His lust for power and possession has caused bloodshed, destruction, and holocaust. The Sufis do not claim a new religion, and although their root is Islam they do not believe in an exclusive religion. They believe in "that mystic religion which, though it has nothing in it but that same spirit, that same truth, and that same life, which always must be the religion of all God's holy angels and saints in heaven, is by the wisdom of this world accounted to be madness."[14]

The Sufis prefer service, meditation, and the ecstasies of mysticism to worldly pleasures. They spend most of their time in meditation and in aiding the poor and needy. They believe that one hour of sincere meditation and help is more precious than a thousand hours of church services. To the Sufi, gold that is not used for feeding the hungry or helping the needy is akin to stone. Every person must constantly exercise his mind and spirit in private, free from anger, malice, and external perception.

Meditation, according to the Sufis, is entering into the very midst of some great truth, so that in the end we are possessed by it. The highest truth is that which we can only realize by plunging into it. Thus, through meditation, the soul is in its true relation to supreme truth, and all actions, words, and behavior become true. Meditation improves our minds with the sense of infinite completeness and emancipation from the world of narrow selfishness.

We meditate upon that adorable energy of the Creator of the Universe and bring into the conscious vision the vastness of the whole universe. Meditation also creates an eternal connection between man and the world, because this world has its other side in our consciousness.

---

[14] Louisa Stuart Costello, *The Rose Garden of Persia, the Sufis.* (London: T. H. Foulis, 1841), pp. 20–21.

God's power emanates and streams forth as consciousness in us and also in the world outside. Thus, meditation means that our consciousness and the vast world outside us are one. Meditation is not taking something to ourselves, but renouncing ourselves, becoming one with all creation. There is, then, no loss, no fear, no pain that can affect us—our relations with our Creator and our fellow creatures become simple, honest, and natural —we are free. This, then, is meditation—to plunge into truth, to live and move and have our being in this.

The fundamental tenet of Sufism is that nothing exists absolutely but God: The human soul is but an emanation from his essence and will finally be restored to him. The primary objective in this transitory state should be a constant approach to the eternal spirit and as perfect a union with divine nature as possible, for which reason worldly attachments must be avoided "as a swimmer, without the impediment of garments, leaves the water with great ease."

Harmony is another source of meditation. It is a cause of existence and the medium between God and man. The peace for which every soul strives is the outcome of harmony. To the Sufi, life without it is unbearable. The attainment of harmony is called heaven and the lack of it, hell. The man who has recognized its importance knows the meaning of an enjoyable life. Harmony, as the fundamental doctrine of the Sufis, signifies that light is for the angels and darkness for the devil. This accord brings order and balance to human life.

Three different kinds of harmony are recognized by the Sufis: eternal, universal, and individual. "Eternal harmony is the harmony of consciousness. As it is in itself eternal, all things and beings live and move in it; yet it remains remote, undisturbed and peaceful. This is the God of the Believer and the God of the Knower."[15]

In this universe, man is drawn in two opposite directions: by the power of harmony toward the infinite and toward manifestation. The infinite is that essential spirit which finally attracts all to itself. The Sufi seeks harmony with the infinite, which he realizes by submission to the will of God, the all-compassionate

---

[15] Inayat Khan, *The Sufi Message*, vol. 8, London: Barrie & Rockliff, 1963, pp. 57–60.

and the all-merciful. God, according to the Sufis, created this universe in which all beings are linked together and attracted to each other with a chord of harmony. The existence of land and water, the attraction between the heavens and the earth all demonstrate this unity.[16]

There are two aspects of individual harmony: the harmony between body and soul and the harmony between individuals. The true joy of the soul is found in love, in beauty, and in service to others. Its outcome is wisdom, calmness, and peace. It is our ego (*Nafs*) that causes all disharmony, first within ourselves and then in others, thus manifesting unruliness in all aspects of life. A Sufi is more interested in the soul's satisfaction because it is more lasting.

"The attainment of harmony in life takes a longer time to acquire and a more careful study than does the training of the ear and the cultivation of the voice, although it is acquired in the same manner as the knowledge of music. To the ear of the Sufi every word spoken is like a note which is true when harmonious and false when inharmonious."

Peoples of every creed, color, class, and race are created as children of God. They are like a strain of music based upon one chord, where the keynote holds many personalities in a single bond of harmony. Man must establish harmony within himself, with others, with the universe, and with the Infinite. He should care neither for blame nor praise. His guiding star should be love. According to Rumi:

> Through love bitter things seem sweet,
> Through love bits of copper are made gold.
> Through love dregs taste like pure wine.
> Through love pains are as healing balms.

The heart of a Sufi is delighted by the sound of the words *love, beauty,* and *harmony*. Nothing in this world can exert so much power on the human heart, mind, and soul as these three words. When we reflect upon this whole creation we cannot fail to see that its purpose is to express these sentiments.

---

[16] Ibid., p. 61.

Every human being suffers from prejudice: He likes one, dislikes another; he esteems one, despises another; but to God we all are alike. We are his children. God is love, and he has created us in his own image. Therefore God, our Father and Creator, is equally pleased with all his creatures. He loves us and therefore cannot be pleased with man's hatred or prejudice. Rumi, in a story concerning Moses and a shepherd whose utterances displeased him, wrote:

A voice came from God to Moses,
"Why hast thou sent my servant away?
Thou has come to draw men to union with me,
Not to drive them far away from me.
So far as possible, engage not in disserving;
The most repugnant to me is divorce.
To each person I have given particular usages.
What is praiseworthy in thee is blamable in him,
What is poison for thee is honey for him.
What is good in him is bad in thee.
I created not men to gain a profit from them,
But to shower my beneficence upon them.
In the men of Hind the usages of Hind are praiseworthy.
In the men of Sind those of Sind.
I regard not the outside and the words,
I regard the inside and the state of heart.
I look at the heart if it be humble,
Though the words may be the reverse of humble.
Because the heart is substance, and the words accidents,
Accidents are only a means, substance is the final cause.
How long wilt thou dwell on words and superficialities?
A burning heart is what I want; consort with burning!
Kindle in thy heart the flame of love,
And burn up utterly thoughts and fine expressions.
No need to turn to the Kaba when one is in it,
And divers have no need of shoes.
The sect of lovers is distinct from all others,
Lovers have a religion and a faith of their own.
Though the ruby has no stamps, what matters it?
Love is fearless in the midst of the sea of fear."[17]

---

[17] Rumi, *The Masnavi*. Abridged and translated by E. Whinfield. (London: The Octagon Press, Ltd., 1973), pp. 82–84.

The Sufi's conception of religion is also unique: Religion may originate in the East or the West, in the South or the North; it may have many denominations and claim millions of followers, yet it will always point to one fact—that all religions and all sects are the expression of beauty and love.

Cross and Christians, from end to end,
I surveyed; He was not on the cross.
I went to the idol-temple, to the ancient pagoda;
No trace was visible there.
I went to the mountains of Herat and Candahar;
I looked; He was not in that hill-and-dale.
With set purpose I fared to the summit of Mount Gaf [Everest];
In that place was only the eagle's habitation.
I bent the reins of search to the Kaba;
He was not in that resort of old and young.
I questioned Avicena of his state;
He was not in Avicena's range.
I fare toward the scene of the high heaven
He was not in that exalted court;
There I saw Him; He was nowhere else.

The Prophet Muhammad says in the Koran:

Love, whether it is human or divine is considered to be the essence of religion and universalism. As it is written in the Bible, God is love. These three words open up a new world and a vast realm for the thinker and the seeker who probes the depth of the secrets of life in search of happiness.

Rumi, referring to love as the real religion and remedy for all maladies of man, states:[18]

The true lover is proved by his pain of heart;
No sickness is there like sickness of heart.
The lover's ailment is different from all ailments;

---

[18] Jalaluddin Rumi, the "pillar" of Sufism and "master" of the Sufis, was born in Balkh in 1207 and died in 1273 in Konia, Turkey. It took him forty-three years to finish his celebrated work, *Masnavi*. During the past seven hundred years, *Masnavi* has been revered and respected as much as the Koran by the Persians and Sufis all over the world.

Love is the astrolabe of God's mysteries.
A lover may hanker after this love or that love,
But at the last he draws to the King of love,
However much we describe and explain love,
When we fall in love we are ashamed of our words.
Explanation by the tongue makes most things clear,
But love unexplained is clearer.
When pen hasted to write,
On reaching the subject of love it split in twain.
When the discourse touched on the matter of love,
Pen was broken and paper torn.

# 3

# The Sufi Ideas of Evolution of Man

I died from the organic realm and became a plant, then I died from the plant life and became an animal. Dying from animality I became a man, so why should I bo afraid of becoming anything less through another death?

Rumi

The Sufis divide the life of the universe into four different stages: the mineral kingdom, the vegetable kingdom, the animal kingdom, and the human kingdom, and of these four domains it is said by the Sufis: "God slept in the mineral period, He dreamed in the vegetable stage, He woke up in the animal age, and He realized Himself in the human era." Underlying this progression is a sense of life that has expressed itself in every step toward the complete development of the human soul and mind.[1]

The best example of this doctrine is found in the work of Rumi, who is an original evolutionary thinker. The only other two thinkers of antiquity who wrote about evolution before Rumi were Plotin and Ibn Miskwaih. Plotin believed in a continuous chain of life, a hierarchy of beings emanating out of original "one," every following stage being lower. But even the lowest, because of its heavenly origin, strives to return to it. "So there is a continuous movement through the universe and a circle of

---

[1] Inayat Kahan, *The Sufi Message*, vol. 7 (London: Barrie & Jenkin, 1962), p. 72.

becoming from the lower to the higher and from the higher to the lower. But this eternal becoming of the world out of God was for Plotin not a process in time; in the realm of appearance he believed in the eternal repetition of an infinite series of similar world periods. However, in the graded continuity of being there is an order and a hierarchy. Every being has its fixed place, and only in its own fixed place it receives its share of life and perfection, which is communicated to it by a being next higher to it and which, in turn, it has to communicate to the one immediately lower than itself."[2]

Ibn Miskwaih believed that a combination of many substances produced the mineral kingdom, which after a long time passed into the lowest form of plant life like grass. Then grass developed into flowers, shrubs, and trees. At this stage some characteristics of animality were evolved, like the distinction of sexes. In the next stage, according to Miskwaih, voluntary motion distinguishes worms from plants. The next stage shows human life in the form of the ape, who gradually develops an erect stature and power of understanding similar to man. Here animality ends and humanity begins.

Rumi was possibly well acquainted with Miskwaih's ideas of evolution. Nothing, for Rumi, is death. Life begins with matter:

The wind, the earth, water and fire are in our service.
For you and me they are dead but as far as God is concerned
    they are alive.[3]

To Rumi, this universe is nothing but an expression and manifestation of ideal. According to him God wanted to manifest himself. He therefore created a mirror whose face is the soul and whose back is the universe. "I created a mirror, whose face is the heart and its back is the world."

To Rumi matter was the first form of existence. It lived as air, fire, wind, and water for a long time, until it entered the next higher stage, that of plant life, later the animal kingdom, and finally the highest form of existence, the human kingdom:

---

[2] Abdul Hakim Khalifa, *The Metaphysics of Rumi* (Lahore, Pakistan: Institute of Islamic Culture, 1965), pp. 33–34.

[3] Rumi, *Masnavi.* Edited and translated by Reynold A. Nicholson, Volume 2, Book 4, Gibb Memorial, London, 1930, p. 472.

He came first to the inorganic realm and then from there it entered the vegetable world. Living for a long time as a plant with no memory of his existence in the inorganic world. Later he rose from the plant to the realm of animality. Again he could not remember his plant life, retaining only an attraction for its beauty in the spring when everything is in full bloom. Being ignorant of the secrets of his evolution, he is like the infant at the breast of his mother who knows not why he is attracted to the breasts.

Then the Creator promoted him from animality to humanity so he evolved from kingdom to the next kingdom until he became wise, intelligent and strong (Homo sapiens). As he has forgotten his former types of intelligence, so soon he will pass beyond this stage. As soon as he abandons his present tendency to greed and avarice then he shall see a thousand other kinds of wisdom.

Sufi's approach to the doctrine of evolution is neither scientific nor theological. It states that there is only one way of rising from lower to the higher stage, and that is by assimilation of the lower into the higher. In the words of Rumi:

From the moment you came into the world of Being,
A ladder was placed before you that you might escape.
First you were mineral, later you turned to plant,
Then you became animal: how should this be a secret of you?
Afterwards you were made man, with knowledge, reason, faith;
Behold the body, which is a portion of dust-pit,
    How perfect it has grown:
When you have travelled on from man, you will doubtless become
    an angel;
After that you are done with this earth: your station is in Heaven.
Pass again even from angelhood: enter that ocean,
That your drop may become a sea which is a hundred seas of
    Oman.
Leave this "son" say ever "one" will your soul;
If your body has aged, what matter, when the soul and (mind)
    is young.[4]

---

[4] Rumi, *Masnavi*, translated by Reynold A. Nicholson.

In another poem Rumi contends:

I died from inorganic matter and was transferred to a plant then I changed from a plant into an animal. I evolved from animality to humanity. Since every evolution has developed me into a better person, why should I be afraid of another death?

In the next stage I shall die from humanity and return as an angel. Then again I shall abandon my angelic personality and become something beyond the imagination. Finally I shall become non-existent when the Divine voice calls me "to return and become one with Him."

In this theory of evolution or creation, Rumi refers to other factors that sounded both new and heretical to his contemporaries. He believed that the cause of the creation was God's irresistible inner necessity. In this theory Rumi anticipated Bergson in the idea that evolution is creative. The *élan vital*, or the will to live a higher and fuller life, creates new organs:

Because without need, the dear God does not give any thing to anyone; if there were no necessity the seven Heavens would not have been created. It was necessity which brought into existence the sun, the moon and the stars. Therefore, necessity is the cause of all existence, and it was this factor which endowed man with all his organs. Since necessity is the cause of creation, O needy one, show your appreciation and gratitude by increasing your need. Almighty showers His beneficence and blessing upon us.[5]

For the Sufi poet's life is nothing but the result of the will to live, to improve and to evolve from a dissatisfied stage into a better world.

Shabastari, the great Sufi poet, describes man's journey from the lowest point to the highest stage of life:

Know first how the perfect man is produced
From the time he is first engendered.

---

[5] Rumi, *Masnavi*, v. 3274–3280, translated by Abdul Hakim Khalifa.

He is produced at first as inanimate matter
Next by the added spirit he is made sentient,
And acquires the motive powers from the Almighty.
Next he is made Lord of will by "The Truth."
In childhood, opens out perception of the world,
And the temptations of the world act upon him
He makes his way from these sources to general notions.
Anger is born in him, and lust of the flesh,
And from these spring avarice, gluttony, pride.
Evil dispositions come into operation.
He becomes worse than an animal, a demon, a brute.
But if from the spirit world there shines a light
From the attraction of grace or reflection of proof,
Then his heart has fellowship with the light of "The truth,"
And he turns back along the road which he came.
From that divine attraction or certain proof
He finds his way to assured faith.
He arises from the seventh hell of the wicked,
He sets his face towards the seventh heaven of the righteous;
Then is he clothed with the quality of repentence,
And is made one chosen among the children of Adam.
He obtains release from his own knowledge,
And like the prophet Jesus he becomes near to God,
He gives up his existence utterly to be plundered,
And in the steps of the "most pure" he ascends
But when his last point is joined to his first,
There is no entrance for angel or for prophet.[6]

Shabastari, in his discussion of man's evolution into perfect man and attainment of unity with God, states:

That man attains to the secrets of unity
Who is not detained at the stages on the road.
But the knower is he that knows very Being,
He that witness Absolute Being,
He recognises no being but very Being,
And being such as his own he gambles clean away
Your being is naught but thorns and weeds,
Cast it all clean away from you.

[6] Shabastari, *Gulshan i Raz*, translated by E. H. Whinfield (London: Trubner Co., 1880), pp. 33–34.

Go sweep out the chamber of your heart,
Make it ready to be the dwelling-place of the beloved.
When you depart out, they will enter in,
In you, void of yourself, will He display His beauty.

Until you cast away obstacles from before you,
The light enters not the chamber of your heart.
As there are four obstacles in this world,
So also the modes of purification from them are four:
First, purification from filthiness of the flesh;
Second, from sin and evil, whispers of the tempers
The third is the purification from bad habits
Which make men as beasts of the field;
The fourth is the purification of the secret
For at this point the pilgrim's journeyings cease,
Whoso is cleansed with these purifications,
Verily he is fit to commune with God.
The principles of a good character are equity,
And thereafter wisdom, temperance, courage.
He who is endued with all these four
Is a sage perfect in thought and deed.
His soul and heart are well informed with wisdom,
He is neither over cunning nor a fool.
By temperance his appetites are subdued,
Intemperance and insensibility alike are banished,
The courageous man is pure from cowardice and rashness.
Equity is as the garment of his nature,
He is void of injustice, thus his character is good.
All the virtues lie in the mean,
Which is alike removed from excess and defect.[7]

Ibn Yamin, the famous Sufi savant of the fourteenth century, referring to man's evolution states:

From the void of non-existence to this dwelling-house
    of clay
I came and rose from stone to plant; but that hath passed
    away.
Thereafter, through the working of the spirit's toil and
    strife,

---

[7] Ibid., pp. 39–40.

I gained, but soon abandoned some lowly form of life:
  That too hath passed away!
In a human breast, no longer a mere unheeding brute,
This tiny drop of Being to a pearl I did transmute
  That too hath passed away!
And the Holy Temple next did I foregather
  with the throng of angels, compassed it about, and
  gazed upon it on;
  That too hath passed away!
Forsaking Ibn Yamin and from His to soaring free,
I abandoned all beside Him so that naught was left.
All else hath passed away![8]

The Persian Sufis having shown the way to scientists of the Western world is a source of national pride and reveals that many aspects of the present civilizations have their roots in the Middle East. There are some differences between Sufis' ideas of evolution and Darwin's theories. The Sufis neither begin nor end with naturalism. Their ideas of matter are not those of the materialists or of the Darwinists. They start with the outer form of the spirit. Darwin ends with man, but the Sufis' end is unlimited. There is also a difference between the Sufis and Darwin about the forces that cause this evolution. Darwin's doctrine of struggle for existence, chance variations, and natural selections find their source in Rumi, who states: "that all life is a battlefield; it is the war of all against all; every atom is struggling with every other form":

This universe is all but a battlefield where atom is struggling against atom as faithful fights the infidel. The source of the present struggle is hidden in the nature of the contradictory principles in our life and our body. There is a verbal struggle, natural struggle and struggle for action. There is contradiction and conflict in different parts of the universe. This universe's existence depends on these conflicts and struggles. To understand this contradiction, take a good look at the different elements of the universe.

[8] Nasrollah S. Fatemi, Faramarz S. Fatemi, and Fariborz S. Fatemi, *Sufism: Message of Brotherhood, Harmony, and Hope* (South Brunswick and New York: A. S. Barnes and Co., Inc., 1976), p. 51.

Creation consists of a struggle of contradictory forces; therefore every element is trying to get advantage. This conflict and contradiction is not only apparent in nature but in your body as well. It is only in the realm of the spirit which peace and harmony is a dominant force. The essence of the soul transcends these contradictions. The nature of spirit is divine. In divinity one finds unity. Conflict begets conflict. Where there is no conflict there is eternity."

We find in Rumi's discourse the seeds of the theory of the survival of the fittest. The superior lives upon the inferior; the former survives and the latter disappears. With Rumi there is no evolution by chance. For him evolution is the result of an ever-increasing need for expansion and assimilation into a higher organism. While Darwin stops at man, Rumi's man evolves to angels and then to God. Rumi's angels are invisible spiritual organisms and his God is the universal spiritual organism with whom man should try to assimilate.

To the Sufis, growth, evolution, assimilation, and unity in this world are manifestations of the form of love. "If there had not been love," according to Rumi, "there would have not been any existence. Had it not been for pure love's sake, how should there have been any reason for the creation of heavens."[9]

While the Greek ideas of love, as stated in one of Plato's dialogues, are craving after immortality in its various forms through procreation and through intellectual and artistic production or through heroic deeds, a movement toward the ideas of perfect beauty, or a mediator between the two worlds, Sufis think of love as an end in itself, as a "divine madness," and directly opposed to the calculated love of the Sophists.

"The fundamental difference between the two schools of thought can be best understood when we examine the relation of rationalism with irrationalism in their respective outlooks on life. Plato was a rationalist in so far as he believed in the knowability of the ground of being through theoretical reason. What he called eternal beauty was nothing but one of the highest ideas or the attractive side of the picture of the eternal truth. But this

---

[9] Rumi, *Masnavi,* quoted by Abdul Hakim Khalifa, p. 37.

truth is objective, impersonal and outside the human soul, only
to be looked at and admired like a perfect piece of art."[10] But
Rumi's idea of love is irrational. In Rumi love and reason are contradictory. Reason for Rumi is a light and a guide, but love is the
goal. The *eros* of Plato is rational and intelligible, but Rumi's
*Ishq* (love) defies any definition or description. Rumi's central
conception is not knowledge of God, but love and assimilation.
Love for Rumi is a paradox in the sense "that in it by giving
we take and by dying we live." The whole course of evolution in
Sufi literature is an illustration of the principle of dying to
live: "There is a unity beyond conception or description between
our Creator and our soul."

The intellect was without direction, and the knower of the spiri-
     tual even than spirit.
No created being is unconnected with Him: that connection is
     indescribable,
Because in the spirit there is no separating and uniting, while
     our thought cannot think except of separating and uniting.
Pursue that which is without separation and union by aid of
     spiritual guide; but the pursuit will not allay your thirst.[11]

Rumi pursues this Sufi argument and states that if it is possible for matter and plant to evolve into man, nothing should,
therefore, stop man to go further to the "all embracing spiritual
organism-God."

Love is an ocean upon which the heavens are
Just a flake of foam; they are like a Zulikha
     madly in love with Joseph.
The wheels of the universe are turned by waves
     of love:
Without love this universe would become inanimate.
How would an inanimate, except through sacrifice,
     change into a plant?
How would vegetable, but by sacrifice, become one
     with spirit of man?

10 Khalifa, *Metaphysics of Rumi*, p. 48.
11 Rumi, *Masnavi*, Ibid., Book 4, v. 3693–97.

> How could the spirit, but through sacrifice, change
> itself into that sacred breath by which Mary
> became pregnant?[12]

The above verses describe Rumi's interpretation of evolution, assimilation, and love (*Ishq*), which are so different from the *eros* of Plato. Plato's argument leads to "the gazing of impersonal intellectual beauty," while Rumi invites us "to be partakers of Infinite Life by becoming living organs in the Life of Life."

There is a squint in the eyes of the intellect, and according to Rumi, "It can never overcome the dualism of the object and subject. It splits reality into two parts and then forgets to unite them. Love to the contrary is above dualism. It integrates, assimilates and then unites them. Unity created by love is beyond description and condition":[13]

> Imperfect intellect is an anathema to love, though it may impress you with its soundness. No matter how clever and wise a man sounds, he is nothing until he abandons his selfishness. Until the angel had abandoned "self", he is a demon. The imperfect intellect sounds like our friend in words and deeds, but when you are in the state of inward feeling it can help you no longer.

Some students of Sufism argue that Sufi ideas of *Ishq* could not be translated into love or *eros*. The word is not definable. Rumi asks this question: "What is love?" Then he answers it: "The sea of Not-Being; there the foot of the intellect is shattered, servitude and sovereignty are known: loverhood is concealed by these two veils. I wish this mortal had a tongue adequate enough to remove the veil of secrecy. Whatever you say or do to remove the veil of secrecy from [*Ishq*], you add another veil upon this mystery."[14]

Sanai, the great mystical poet (d. 1131), in discussing perfect love, states:

---

[12] Rumi, *Masnavi*, p. 196.
[13] Khalifa, *Metaphysics of Rumi*, p. 44.
[14] Rumi, *Masnavi*. Vol. 3, v. 4723–26.

Who would be loved, let him possess
   A true beloved like mine,
And share in secret blessedness
   Love's mystery divine:
Lovers like us none else, I guess,
   Are found in earth's confine.
"Soul of the world"—such was the name
   My idol gave to me;
While I do live, her I proclaim
   Soul of my world to be,
And none I know doth own the same
   Dear loyalty as she.

That heart which stands aloof from pain and woe
No seal or signature of Love can show:
Thy Love, thy love I chose, and as for wealth,
If wealth be not my portion, be it so!
For wealth, I ween, pertaineth to the world;
Ne'er can the world and love together go!
So long as Thou dost dwell within my heart
Ne'er can my heart become the thrall of woe.[15]

---

[15] Sanai, translated by Edward G. Browne, *Literary History of Persia*. Vol. II (London: T. Fisher Unwin, 1906), p. 322.

# 4

## Love in Sufi's Lexicon

Everything except love was devoured by love:
To the beak of bird of love the two worlds are but a single
grain.

Rumi

You walk on the water, so does a piece of wood,
You fly in the air, so does a bird,
You travel to the Kaaba in a single night, so does a conjurer,
The true man attaches his heart to none but Love.

Abu Yazid Bastami

Sufis speak of three kinds of love:

1. Divine love (*Ishqi Ilahi*), which is on the one hand the love of the Creator for the creature in which he creates himself, and on the other hand it is the love of creature for his Creator;

2. Spiritual love (*Ishqi Ruhani*), found in the creature who is always in quest of the Being whose image he discovers in himself is love that has no other concern, aim, or will than to be adequate to the Beloved;

3. Natural love (*Ishqi Tabiy*), which desires to possess and seek the satisfaction of its own desires without concern for the satisfaction of the Beloved. "And that, alas," say the Sufis, "is how most people understand love today."

The real problem according to Ibn Arabi, the prominent Sufi mentor, is to find a way to reconcile spiritual love with physical love; only when the two aspects of creatural love have been reconciled can one ask whether a conjunction is possible between it and the divine love that is love in its true essence.

In Rumi's words, love puts reason to silence:

> Love is a perfect muzzle of evil suggestions;
> Without love whoever succeeded in stopping them?
> Be a lover, and seek that fair Beauty,
> Hunt for that waterfowl in every stream!
> How can you get water from that which cuts it off?
> How can you gain understanding from what destroys
>     understanding?
> Love of God cuts short reasonings, O beloved,
> For it is a present refuge from perplexities.
> Through love bewilderment befalls the power of speech,
> It no longer dares to utter what passes;
> For if it sets forth an answer, it fears greatly
> That its secret treasure may escape its lips.
> Therefore it closes lips from saying good or bad,
> So that its treasure may not escape it.

A perfect man, by Sufi standards, combines all three forms of love. He is the final goal of evolution and the whole world is built around him. Rumi states:

> In appearance man is the microcosm, but in reality he is the macrocosm. We assume that the branch of the tree is the producer of the fruit, forgetting that the real cause of the existence of the tree's branch is to bring to us its fruits. If there were no hope for the production of the fruit, the gardener would never plant the root of the tree. Therefore, in reality the planting of the tree is for the sake of the fruit, although the appearance is different.

The prophet Muhammad declares:

We are the last but the foremost.

But the Sufis' description of this ideal man is contradictory:

Man is small, yet he is everything.

Sadi, referring to this state of man, exclaims:

> Man's state is that of changing lightning
> One moment it appears and at another vanishes.
> We are sometimes sitting in high heaven:
> On another occasion we cannot see the back of our foot.

Were a Sufi always to remain in the state of grace, he would desire the pleasures of neither this nor the next world.

In declaring his identity with God, Bayazid often describes himself "as a humble creature without a will, thought or even movement, dependent on the loving God." They all believed in a world where man through love is everything, yet at times is helpless.

> Man in appearance is a small part of the world but in reality he is the world. Physically a fly can knock him down with pain, but mentally his mind encompasses the seven heavens [universe].

Shible Numani, referring to the nature of man:

> The mind of the man is greater than the universe. He is characterized by two contradictory terms: *Nafs* (selfishness) and *Ruh* (soul).

> This is the same as the old Zoroastrian idea of evil and goodness, the former representing the principles of darkness in man's character, and the latter the divine virtue and light. The Sufis like Zoroastrians believe that eventually light conquers darkness and therefore, lower self of man can be destroyed by the realization of truth and by "moral purification" (*Mujahida*).

Belief in the realization of divine love is responsible for the Sufi conception of the "perfect man," which has not only played an important role in the Sufis' views about God and man but established the basis of the fundamental kinship between Shiism of Iran and Sufism: All esoterism in Shiism and Sufism recognizes a divine manifestation of love in human form. There is the exaltation of the prophets on the one hand and the deification of saints on the other, but the Shiahs go hand in hand with the Sufi conception of the ideal man in search of divine love. The ideal man, therefore, is hardly distinguishable from God. His heart is the throne of God and his intellect the pen of destiny; his soul is the preserved ground for the love of the almighty. At this stage, according to the Sufis, man can claim his identity with God. He is like a tree sprung from the Divine Root. The Koran very clearly refers to this closeness between man and his God: "In our own image we created man."

Rumi says about the ideal man:

> The man of clay got knowledge from God and then he was raised to Seventh Heaven. Human knowledge is only the means, the love of God is the end. The ideal man possesses two kinds of knowledge, one acquired through education and experience, the other is the gift of God whose source is man's heart and soul. When man is the privileged of recognizing and acquiring the latter, all the secrets of life and creation would be revealed to him. It is at this stage that no words however eloquent and elaborate could describe the divine qualities of the ideal man. The heart and the book of Sufi is not darkened by words. It is a heart as white as snow. The one whose heart is impressionless and clean, he becomes a mirror of the secrets of the unseen.

Instead of understanding the spirit of love and universalism, man has used religion and nationality to distinguish himself from others. Importance is given to the name of a particular prophet, his book, his church, his priests or clergy. Prominence is attributed to Moslem, Hindu, Jew, or Christian. Loyalty to a particular creed or nation leads to discrimination or dislike of other religions and nations. It is in this way that conflict and war arise.

Human rights are infringed upon when the violation affects our co-religionist, race or compatriots. Then we demonstrate, protest, and complain, while our conscience is never bothered when the same violation is oppressing and destroying others. It is a tribal world where each tribe and clan selfishly is concerned about its own narrow interest while ignoring the injustice in other communities. We all forget that peace and justice are indivisible. The only way to obtain and maintain them is to think and act in global and universal terms. The fight for justice and peace has to go beyond borders, race, color, and creed. It has to encompass the whole of mankind.

Nature, according to the Sufis, expresses the universal religion, which has the same spirit, the same truth, and the same life, which always has and always will rule this universe.

> Abandon your selfish identity and settle in universal
> love and unity, forever;
> God is cup-bearer and the wine;
> He knows what manner of love is mine.
> All these gold wares on the table of heaven
> Are in order that one day we'll be bidden to its feast.

> What is to be done, O Moslems, for I do not recognize
> myself.
> I am neither Christian, nor Jew, nor Zoroastrian, nor
> Moslem.
> I am not of the East, nor of the West, nor of the land,
> nor of the sea;
> I am not of nature's mint, nor of the circling heavens,
> I am not of earth, nor of water, nor of air, nor of fire;
> I am not of the empyrean, nor of the dust nor of existence,
> not of entity.
> I am not of India, nor of China, nor of Bulgaria, nor
> of Sagsin;
> I am not of this world, nor of the next, nor of Paradise
> nor of the Hell;
> I am not of Adam, nor of Eve, nor of Eden and Rizwan.
> My place is the placeless, my trace is the traceless;
> Tis neither body nor soul, but I belong to the soul of
> the beloved.[1]

Man differs from other species because of human qualities. These are not drinking, eating, sleeping, or love-making. Human qualities can be developed only through love and service to our fellow men.

---

[1] Rumi, *Masnavi*, translated by Reynold Nicholson. Quoted by Fatemi in *Sufism*, p. 106.

The development of love is often hindered by our selfishness and greed. We love people because they help or love us. We trade love for love. The Sufis believe that, to love is to give, forgive, sacrifice, and suffer. One should love because that is humane. Love means patience, understanding, magnanimity, gentleness, and devotion. Greed and selfishness destroy these qualities. Rumi, alluding to this selfishness which is the cause of hatred and conflict, writes:

> Once a man came and knocked at the door of his friend. His friend said, "What art thou, O faithful one?" He said, " 'Tis I." He answered "There is no admittance. There is no room for the immature at my royal feast.
>
> Naught but fire of separation and absence,
> Can cook the raw one and free him from hypocrisy!
> Since thy 'self' has not yet left thee,
> Thou must be burned in fiery flames."

> The poor man went away, and for one whole year journeyed burning with grief for his friend's absence. His heart burned till it was cooked; then he went again and drew near to the house of his friend. He knocked at the door in fear and trepidation lest some careless word might fall from his lips. His friend shouted "Who is that at the door?" He answered "This is thou who art at the door, O beloved." The friend said "Since 'tis I, let me come in. There is not room for two 'I's in one house."

Would you have eyes and ears of reason clear,
Tear off the obstructing veil of greed!
The blind imitation of that Sufi proceeded from greed;
Greed closed his mind to the pure light.
Yea, it was greed that took astray that Sufi, and
Brought him to loss of property and ruin. Greed of
Victuals, greed of that ecstatic singing hindered his wits from
    grasping the truth.
If greed stained the face of a mirror,
That mirror would be as deceitful as we men are!
If a pair of scales were greedy of riches,

Would they tell truly the weight of anything?
I will tell you a tale; hearken attentively
That you may know how greed closes up the ears.
Every man subject to greed is a miser.
Can eyes or hearts clouded with greed see clearly,
The illusion of rank and riches blinds his sight,
Like hair dropping down before his eyes.[2]

"Man," having been created in the image of God, enjoys the best stature according to the Koran, and being the greatest of God's creations, can attain divine attributes only by fulfilling his mission on earth: "He should clean his heart of malice and hatred and follow the path of service and love."

The aim of the Sufis is to reach this stage of purity, decency, and selflessness. The means of achieving it is through harmony between action and contemplation; balance between material desires and intellectual and spiritual objectivity. The Sufis believe that their theories and practices can assist this confused and confusing world in becoming a more harmonious and happy place. The Sufi's function is to remind man of his nature and his purpose in life so that he can seek all that he needs within himself. Hafiz, the great Sufi poet, referred to this aim.

# I

Long years my heart had made request
Of me, a stranger, hopefully
(Not knowing that itself possessed
The treasure that is sought of me),
That Jamshid's chalice I should win
And it would see the world therein.
That is a pearl by far too rare
To be contained within the shell
Of time and space; lost vagrants there
Upon the ocean's margin, well
We know it is a vain surmise
That we should hold so great a prize.

---

[2] Ibid., p. 160.

## II

There was a man that loved God well;
In every motion of his mind
God dwelt; and yet he could not tell
That God was in him, being blind:
Wherefore as if afar he stood
And cried, "Have mercy, O my God!"

## III

This problem that had vexed me long
Last night unto the taverner
I carried; for my hope was strong
His judgement sure, that could not err,
Might swiftly solve infallibly
The riddle that had baffled me.

I saw him standing in his place,
A goblet in his grasp, a smile
Of right good cheer upon his face,
As in the glass he gazed awhile
And seemed to view in vision clear
A hundred truths reflected there.

## IV

"That friend who, being raised sublime
Upon the gallows, glorified
The tree that slew Him for his crime,
This was the sin for which He died,
That, having secrets in His charge,
He told them to the world at large."

So spake he; adding, "But the heart
That has the truth within its hold
And, practising the rosebud's art,
Conceals a mystery in each fold,
That heart hath well this comment lined
Upon the margin of the mind.

"When Moses unto Pharaoh stood,
The men of magic strove in vain
Against his miracle of wood;
So every subtlety of brain
Must surely fail and feeble be
Before the soul's supremacy.

"And if the Holy Ghost descend
In grace and power infinite
His comfort in these days to lend
To them that humbly wait on it,
Theirs too the wondrous works can be
That Jesus wrought in Galilee."

## V

"What season did the Spirit wise
This all-revealing cup assign
Within thy keeping?" "When the skies
Were painted by the Hand Divine
And heaven's mighty void was spanned,
Then gave He this into my hand."

"Yon twisted coil, yon chain of hair
Why doth the lovely Idol spread
To keep me fast and fettered there?"
"Ah, Hafiz!", so the wise man said,
"'Tis a mad heart, and needs restraint
That speaks within thee this complaint."[3]

Sufi teachings revolve around the two fundamental doctrines of the transcendent unity of being (*Wahdat al wujud*) and the universal or perfect man (*al insan al-Kamil*): "Man is the only creature in this world who is centrally and axially located so that he reflects the Divine names and qualities and conscious manner."

The Sufi's purpose is none other than the realization of the state of this union with God. Through the universal man God

---

[3] A. J. Arberry, *Hafiz* (Cambridge: University Press, 1947), pp. 97–99.

contemplates himself and all things that he has brought into being.[4]

Rabia, one of the founders of the Sufi order, pleads:

> O God, whatsoever Thou hast apportioned to me of worldly things, do Thou give that to Thy enemies; and whatsoever Thou hast apportioned to me in the world to come, give that to Thy friends; for Thou sufficest me in Hell, and if I worship Thee for fear of Hell, burn me in Hell, and if I worship Thee in hope of Paradise, exclude me from Paradise; but if I worship Thee for Thy own sake, grudge me not Thy everlasting beauty.[5]

Abu Yazid Bastami (d. A.D. 877) says:

> God had compassion on me. He granted me eternal knowledge, and put into my throat a tongue of his goodness. He created for me an eye out of His Light, and I saw all creatures through God. With the tongue of His Goodness I communed with God, and from the knowledge of God I acquired a knowledge, and by His Light I gazed on Him.
>
> Lord God, let me not be deluded by this. Let me not become self-satisfied with my own being, not to yearn for Thee. Better it is that Thou shouldst be mine without me, than that I should be my own without Thee.
>
> I gazed upon God with the eye of certainty after that He had advanced me to the degree of independence from all creatures, and illumined me with His Light, revealing to me the wonders of His secrets and manifesting to me the grandeur of His Person.

By saying "Glory be to me," Abu Yazid angered many but revealed himself as a man of profound spirituality. Through lengthy meditation and austerity Abu Yazid reached a state of compelling awareness of the merging of his human individuality into the individuality of God.

The introduction of "intoxication" into the Sufi doctrine is attributed to Abu Yazid. In this respect he differs from the "so-

---

[4] Hussein Nasr, *Sufi Essays* (Albany: State Univ. of New York Press, 1972), p. 35.
[5] Rabia, quoted by R. Nicholson.

ber" school of Baghdad, headed by Al Jonaid (d. 910). Jonaid studied the work of Abu Yazid and reached the same conclusion regarding mystical experience and transformation of personal ego into the eternal ego; but he shrouded his expressions in cautious terms and supported his arguments by skillful "neo-Platonic" interpretations of key quotations from the Koran and traditions of the Prophet Muhammad. His phrasing was that "God makes thee die to thyself and become resurrected in Him."

Jonaid also contends that the highest virtue of man is truthfulness, which means abhorrence of false tendencies and hypocrisy. The end of Sufism is to become one with truth (Al Hagg). It is at this stage that man's soul becomes cleansed of the impurity of mind, heart, and soul. He possesses nothing and is not possessed by anybody or any worldly ambition.

> Love is a sea that hath not any shore,
>     and help upon that shoreless sea is none;
> Who sails it sets his eyes on land no more;
>     yet gladly am I on that voyage gone—
>     for Ah! how good it is to sail that sea!
> What though the longest trip at last be o'er,
>     my love is on the same big ship with me,
>     and when she drowns, I drown.
>
> Talk not of reason to a man in love,
>     nor pity thy arguments against good wine,
> Love has a wisdom, wisdom cannot prove—
>     reason knows nothing of things Divine.
>
> The happy heart can find its happy way,
>     nor its direction need of any ask;
> I charge thee fill each moment of the day
>     with love, as wine fills to the neck the flask.
> None but pure ages may see the face I love,
>     scarcely discernible, as the young moon
> That like a spirit yonder walks above
>     the sleeping trees with little silver shoon.
>
> Beloved, it is not for you to question the words
>     of the wise,

To say, "such and such is not so," or, "it seems
    not good in my eyes,"
Attend to your beauty, Beloved: It is that your
    business lies.

To neither this world nor the next will I bow down
    this dream-filled head—
Ah, blessed be heaven that it put such dreams,
    such dreams, in my head!
But my heart—ah, what of my heart and its agony
    shall be said!

What is it inside my heart that cries out night
    and day?
It is not the voice of my soul—that hath never
    a word to say;
But something laments in my heart in a tossed
    tempestuous way.

Never that heart was set on the wealth of the
    world and its ways
One thing have I asked of this life—to look day
    and night in your face;
My wealth was the thought of you, and my fame
    was the hope of your praise.[6]

For centuries, there has been an argument between the religious groups and the lovers of Sufi poetry, whether the words
*wine* and *love* used by some Sufi poets are the wines of the spirit
and the love of God, or whether they refer to real wine and physical love in this world.

The orthodox Muslim regards the Sufi poetry in much the
same light as the orthodox Jew or Christian regards the Song of
Solomon or the divine love-story of Dante. They all say: "These
are not love-songs, but 'divine and spiritual allegory.'" Richard
Le Galienne, an accomplished scholar of Persian and Sufi poetry,
refutes this argument and states that the orthodox view may be
correct about some Sufi poets but not about all of them: "As with
Omar Khayyam, the question of the literal or symbolic meanings
of the epicureanism of Hafiz has, of course, been raised, and

---

[6] Hafiz, translated by Richard Le Gallienne.

answered in the same way. Some still have it that the wine of
Hafiz was the wine of the spirit, and the love he celebrates was
the love of God. There is a type of mind which always prefers to
interpret masterpieces after this fashion—abstract intelligences,
with a holy horror of flesh and blood, who love to dehumanize
literature, and prose—our great warm-hearted classic Cyptograms
of fantastic philosophy or speculation. We need go no further
than the Bible for an illustration."[7]

Just as our theologians tried to hide the beauty of the Song
of Solomon by attaching to it a Christian interpretation, so the
Persians have sought to cannonize Hafiz's book (the Divan);
but Hafiz himself sings a different song:

> When thus I sit with roses in my breast,
> Wine in my hand, and the beloved kind;
> I ask no more—the world can take the rest.
> Even the Sultan's self is, to my mind,
> On such a planetary night as this,
> Compared with me a veritable slave.

> Two gallons of old wine, and two old friends
> That know the world and well each other know,
> A corner of the meadow, an old book,
> A river's flow:
> In such simplicity begins and ends—
> All that I ask of God—keep all the rest,
> Luxurious world, but leave me this green nook;
> I keep the best.

> The winds of March blow up the clouds of spring,
> Heavy with flowers—O thou new-born year!
> I, like thyself, am feign to dance and sing;
> But where, O where
> Shall I money find for wine and string?

> Out on my empty purse! Didst ever see
> In any other spring such girls as those!
> They have bright eyes for everyone but me:
> Red little rose—
> O for the money to buy one kiss from thee!

[7] Richard Le Gallienne, *Odes from the Divan of Hafiz* (London: Duckworth & Co.,
1905), pp. XXIV–V.

# 5

## The Ideal Man

Sufism is liberty, so that a man is freed from the bonds of desire; self-conceit, anger and hatred.

Hassan Nuri

Learn from yon orient shell to love thy foe,
And store with pearls the hand, that brings thee woe;
Free, like yon rock, from base vindictive pride,
Emblaze with gems the wrist, that rends thy side.

Hafiz

To the Sufis, purification of the mind is as necessary as cleansing the body. Impurity of mind causes more diseases than any germ. To be spiritual is to be natural. Great religious leaders attained greatness not because of working miracles or seeing strange and wonderful phenomena, but through living simple, pure, and natural lives.

Mental purification, according to the Sufis, could be accomplished in two ways:

First, the mind may be purified through true transcendental meditation. Lack of thinking and excess activities of the mind result in mental impurities. Regular meditation removes impurities, gives us the opportunity to think and to remove any impure thoughts. If the mind is constantly disturbed, one seldom receives intuition, inspiration, or useful ideas.

The second way of purifying the mind is by adopting the right attitude in our relations to the world and its people. We may meditate or sit in silence in different postures, but if our attitude toward life is cynical, aloof, or bitter, the mind can never be purified.

How does one achieve the right attitude? The first lesson is recognition of our shortcomings and our helplessness. This helps us to avoid hasty judgment and unconstructive criticism of others. It is so easy to find fault, to dislike, and to hate. Most of us are under the illusion that we are blameless—that it is the other person who should be blamed for what is wrong. We forget that "the one who blames most becomes most blameworthy."

There is no perfect man or woman in this world. It is only the comparison that makes us think that one person is better or worse. In Rumi's words, "there are no absolutes, there are only relatives; and we must learn to get along with relatives. Everything is judged by comparison. There is some good in the worst of us and some evil in the best of us." Thus we should get away from our pompous and hypocritical attitude of finding fault with our neighbors and forgetting our own great errors. There are other persons than ourselves in this world; and their ideas, their feelings, and their points of view should be respected. Reality is a dome of many-colored glass, and from his little corner each of us sees a different combination of colors in the kaleidoscope. The word *truth* is only the common denominator of our delusions, and certainly it would be a great error to believe that we are its only guardian in this world. The purification of the mind, from a moral point of view, may be achieved by observing our own shortcomings, by looking at others as we look at ourselves, and by putting ourselves in the position of others instead of accusing them of immoralities and infirmities.

Omar Khayyam comments on the hypocrisy of righteous people:

> Oh thou who burn'st in heart for those who
> Burn in Hell, whose fires thyself shall feed in turn,
> How long be crying, mercy on them God!
> Why, who art thou to teach, and he to learn.
> Oh City Magistrate, you go more astray

Than I, although to drinking I give way;
I drink the blood of grapes, you that of men:
Which of us the more bloodthirsty, pray?
Was ever man born who never went astray?
Did ever mortal pass a sinless day?
If I do ill and Thou requite with ill,
Wherein does our behavior differ, pray?

Rumi, referring to the Sufi doctrine of tolerance and respect for all ideas, creeds, and faiths, states that all doctrines contain an element of truth:

Just so every one in matters of doctrine
Gives a different description of the hidden subject.
A philosopher expounds it in one way,
And a critic at once refutes his proposition.
A third censures both of them;
A youth spends his life in traducing the others.
Every one mentions indications of this road,
In order to create an impression that he has gone it.
This truth and that truth cannot be all true,
And yet all of them are not entirely astray in error,
Because error occurs not without some truth,
Fools buy base coins from their likeness to real coins.
If there were no genuine coins current in the world,
How could coiners succeed in passing false coins?
If there were no truth, how could falsehood exist?
Falsehood derives its plausibility from truth.
Say not, then, that all these creeds are false,
The false ones ensnare hearts by scent of truth.
Say not that they are all erroneous fancies,
There is no fancy in the universe without some truth.
He who accepts everything as true is a fool,
And he who says all is false is a knave.[1]

Purification of the mind, in the Sufi's world, means purging ourselves of all undesirable thoughts, words, and acts. Purity does not create phenomena but is a phenomenon itself. When the heart is pure it projects the light of the soul just as the light is projected from a searchlight.

---

[1] E. H. Whinfield, *Musnavi Manavi* (London: Octave Press, 1973), pp. 98–99.

The mind is a storehouse of all the knowledge that one has accumulated by studies, by experience, by intuition, and by impression through any of the five senses. Mental purification, therefore, is the only method by which one can reach the spiritual goal. At this stage man is considered closer to God than any other creatures.

Rumi tells the story of how God made man (Adam) superior to the angels in wisdom and honor:

He said, "By God, who knoweth hidden secrets,
Who created pure Adam [man] out of dust;—
In the form, three cubits high, which he gave him,
He displayed the contents of all spirits, all decrees!
Communicated to him the indelible tablet of existence,
All that should be first and last to endless eternity
He taught him, with the knowledge of his own 'names',
So that the angels were beside themselves at his instruction,
And gained more sanctity from his sanctification.
The expansion of their minds, which Adam brought about,
Was a thing unequalled by the expansion of the heavens.
For the wide expanse of that pure mind
The wide space of the seven heavens was not enough."
The Prophet said that God has declared,
"I am not contained in aught above or below,
I am not contained in earth or sky, or even in highest heaven,
Know this for surety, O beloved!
Yet am I contained in the believer's heart!
If ye seek me, search in such hearts!"
He said also, "Enter the hearts of my servants[2]
To gain the paradise of beholding Me, a fearer of God."
Highest heaven, with all its light and wide expanse,
When it beheld Adam, was shaken from its place!
Highest heaven is greatness itself revealed;
But what is form when reality draws nigh?
Every angel declared, "In times of yore
We bore friendship to the plains of earth;
We were wont to sow the seed of service on the earth,
Wherefore we bore a wondrous attachment to it.
What was this attachment to that house of earth
When our own natures are heavenly?

---

[2] Koran 89:29.

What was the friendship of lights like us to darkness?
How can light dwell together with darkness?
O Adam! that friendship arose from the scent of thee,
Because the earth is the warp and weft of thy body.
Thy earthly body was taken from there,
Thy pure spirit of light was shed down from here![3]

But our souls were enlightened by thy spirit[4]
Long, long before earth had diverted it to itself.
We used to be on earth, ignorant of the earth,—
Ignorant of the treasure buried within it.
When we were commanded to depart from that place,
We felt sorrow at turning our steps away from it.
So that we raised many questions, saying,
'O Lord! Who will come to take our place?
Wilt Thou barter the glory of our praises and homage
For the vain babble [of men]?'
The commands of God then diffused joy upon us; He said
'What are ye saying at such length?
What ye give tongue to so foolishly
Is as the words of spoiled children to their father.
I knew of myself what ye thought,
But I desired that ye should speak it;
As this boasting of yours is very improper,
So shall my mercy be shown to prevail over my wrath:
O Angels, in order to show forth that prevailing,
I inspired that pretension to cavil and doubt;
If you say your say, and I forbear to punish you,
The gainsayers of my mercy must hold their peace.
My mercy equals that of a hundred fathers and mothers;
Every soul that is born is amazed thereat.
Their mercy is as the foam of the sea of my mercy;
It is mere foam of waves, but the sea abides ever!
What more shall I say? In that earthly shell
There is naught but foam of foam of foam of foam!' "
God is that foam; God is also that pure sea,
For His words are neither a temptation nor a vain boast.

---

[3] Rumi, *Masnavi*, translated by Whinfield.
[4] The Logos, the first of created beings, was afterwards embodied in Adam, the "Perfect Man," or Microcosm.

The purpose of Sufism is to enable man to realize his ability and dignity and to set his soul free from the shackles of ego, greed, and prejudice. Sufism alerts man to the fact that answers to his salvation are not in outwardly religious pretensions. It reminds him to seek all that he needs inwardly within himself, to tear his attachment from the world of corruption, prejudice, hatred, and conflict. It removes man from his lowest to the highest state in order to reinstate him in his primordial perfection.

At this stage man is awakened to the true nature of the Creator, the nature of man and the spiritual values, which help man to becoming the total theophany of God's attributes.

Rumi, in the following story, explains how God prefers the service and inwardly virtues to outwardly and conventional worship:

The celebrated Sufi, Abu Yazid of Bastam, in Khorasan, who lived in the third century of Hijra, was making a pilgrimage to Mecca, and visiting all the "pillars of insight" who lived in the various towns that lay on his route. At last he discovered the "Saint of the Age" in the person of a venerable Dervish, with whom he held the following conversation:

The sage said, "Whither are you going, O Bayazid?
Where will you bring your caravan to halt?"
Bayazid replied, "At dawn I start for the Kaba."
Quoth the sage, "What provision for the way have you?"
He answered, "I have two hundred silver dirhams;
See them tied up tightly in the corner of my cloak?"

The sage said "Circumambulate me seven times;
Count this better than circumambulating the Kaba;
And as for the dirhams, give them to me, O liberal one,
And know you have finished your course and obtained your
    wish.
You have made the pilgrimage and gained the life to come,
You have become pure, and that in a moment of time.
Of a truth that is God which your soul sees in me,
For God has chosen me to be His house.
Though the Kaba is the house of His grace and favour

Yet my body too is the house of His secret
Since he made that house He has never entered it,
But none but that living one enters this house!
When you have seen me you have seen God,
And have circumambulated the veritable Kaba.
To serve me is to worship and praise God;
Think not that God is distinct from me.
Open clear eyes and look upon me,
That you may behold the light of God in a mortal.
The Beloved once called the Kaba 'My House,'
But has said to me 'O my servant' seventy times,
O Bayazid you have found the Kaba,
You have found a hundred precious blessings,"
Bayazid gave heed to these deep sayings,
And placed them as golden earrings in his ears.[5]

Shaikh Abdullah Ansari, a great Sufi mentor, alluding to this "state" of man explains:

> The heart inquired of the soul
> What is the beginning of approach to truth
> What is it and, and what is its fruit?
> The soul answered:
> The beginning of it is the annihilation of ego,
> Its end absolute submission,
> And its fruit is immortality.

The Sufis believe that there is a covenant between God and man by virtue of which man is assured peace of mind and inward happiness as long as he remains truly human. The man who reaches this stage is close to divinity. Hafiz of Shiraz states:

Deep in my heart there dwells a holy bird;
O but 'tis weary of its earthly cage,
And in the dark of the body sadly sings;
    Its heritage
Is the ninth heaven; its right is to be heard
Before high God; its royal nest should be
For wide as the empyrean are its wings—the Sidra tree.
When from the dunghill of this world it flies,

---

[5] Whinfield, *Musnavi Manavi*, pp. 88–89.

Bird of the soul, it stays not in its flight
Till on the top of heaven it proudly stands, far out of sight
Of the said straining of our mortal eyes;
And wheresoever its rainbow shadows rest,
The folk go happy in those favored lands
From East to West.
This earth, the lonely footstool of the stars,
Is not thy place, O Hafiz; nay such songs
Should fill the listening palaces of heaven;
To God belongs
Thy voice, sweet bird, behind these fleshly bars;
Thy singing pastures are those fields on high,
Heaven's roses and the dew that falls in heaven
Bird of the sky.

In assessing the philosophy of the Persian Sufi poets, one must bear in mind the fusion of Persian classical ideas and Islam. In the Persian classical ideas several concepts run through their thinking. The first thought was the idea of concordia. For the Sufis, concord was cosmic. The goal of spiritual man is to journey through the cosmos and seek the means through which man can get his bearings through this journey. Sufi cosmology takes its root both from the Stoics' concord, and the immanent rationalism of Islam. It is a map of the universe that one must possess if he is seeking his spiritual destination. Sufi cosmology, therefore, deals with ideas that hold dissident elements in harmony. It can be discerned in the harmonies of music, in the movements of the heavenly bodies, in the behavior of animals. "The sun graciously gives way at night to the weaker stars and moon, and even by day suffers himself to be eclipsed or shrouded by cloud or mist. The stars in turn show each other consideration and preserve their orbits without collision. Likewise in the lower world the birds rest beside the birds, the ants assist the ants, and the bees do not quarrel over the same flower."[6] Man, of all creatures, being endowed with reason, speech, laughter, and tears, is best able to perceive the harmony of the universe and resolve his differences in reasonable ways.

Rumi explains this theory in the following verses:

---

[6] Dion of Prusa; quoted in *Erasmus of Christendom*, by Roland Baitan.

What worlds the principle of reason embraces
How broad in this ocean of reason
Yea, the reason of man is a boundless ocean.
O son, that ocean requires, as it were a diver
On this fair ocean our human forms
Float about, like bowls on the surface of water;
Yea, like cups on the surface, till they are filled;
And then filled, these cups sink into the water.
The ocean of reason is not seen; reasoning men are seen;
But our minds are only as waves or spray thereof.

Sufi cosmology also deals not with the quantitative aspects
of things as is the case in modern science, but with their quali-
tative and symbolic aspects. It also casts a light upon things so
that they become worthy subjects of contemplation, lucid and
transparent, losing their habitual opaqueness and darkness. The
primary function of Sufi cosmology and science of nature is to
provide a prototype of the cosmos for the traveler upon the path
of truth and to provide interrelation between man and nature.[7]

In connection with the ideal personality of man, the Sufis
developed the theory of prophethood and its medium knowledge
of revelation. This was contradictory to the Orthodox Muslim
conception, which believed prophethood to be the highest status
of man and the last of the prophets, Muhammad, as "the seal
of the prophets" with whom the door of prophethood and revelation was closed.

The Sufis abandoned this orthodox belief and introduced the
idea that the ideal man or saint is superior to the prophet. In
order to avoid the wrath and anger of the Orthodox Muslims they
claimed that Muhammad was first a saint and then the prophet
of Allah. Prophethood, according to the Sufis, is double faced;
one face toward the Creator and the other toward the creature;
but sainthood has only one face, the face of God.

"The saints were clothed with all the attributes of the prophethood, except the promulgation of the law; otherwise, under a disguised terminology, everything special to the prophets reappeared
in the saints."

Ghazali, the spokesman of orthodoxy as well as of mysti-

---

[7] Hussein Nasr, *Sufi Essays* (Albany: State Univ. of New York Press, 1972), p. 46.

cism, had taken an important step in developing a theory of prophetic consciousness as a stage in the development of the human mind. It is a characteristic of philosophy as well as of mysticism to bring out the universal from the particular and the historical, a tendency directly opposed to the dogmatic interpretation of positive religion. This feature of rationalism and mysticism asserted itself in Ghazali. The view of Rumi is fundamentally the same as that of Ghazali but, in order to appreciate their agreement and difference, let us first study Ghazali's own words:

> Believing in prophethood means to acknowledge that there is a stage above reason in which an eye is opened that has perception special to it which reason is incapable of comprehending as the ear is incapable of perceiving the colors.

> And who has not been granted a little taste of mysticism, his knowledge of the reality prophethood is no more than the words.[8]

Then Al-Ghazali, on the basis of personal experience, which is considered a piece of valuable religious psychology, states:

> The life of reason develops genetically and chronologically after the life of the senses but transcends the data of the senses in a way that there is nothing common between the universal categories of the reason and the data of the senses. Prophetic revelation is the produce of an ultrarational faculty which is latent in man. Who can deny the different grades of development of natural reason in different people? If reason were equally developed in everybody, all would have understood the sciences equally well and the difference between the dull and the intelligent would not exist. To one even a long teaching does not make this thing clear and to the other only a hint is sufficient. Another one is so perfect that ideas spring from his mind without having been taught by anybody as God said "its oil gives light although no fire touched it—Light upon Light," and that is an analogy for the prophets. Subtle things are uncovered to their inner eye, things that they never learned from

---

[8] Abdul Hakim Khalifa, *The Metaphysics of Rumi* (Lahore, Pakistan: Institute of Islamic Culture. 1965). pp. 101–2.

others. That is called inspiration and the Holy prophet meant this when he said that "the Holy Ghost breathes it into my mind."[9]

It is important to understand Al-Ghazali's point of view that it is possible to realize prophethood through mystic experience and search for truth. However, he refrains from giving us his views as to the question whether it is a faculty latent in every human being or that, as the Orthodox Muslims believe, God only gives this power to a few men chosen to be prophets. This prophethood ended with Muhammad.

On the other side of this argument we find Rumi more frank and more logical. He first accepts Al-Ghazali's theory that prophethood is higher than rational self and is capable of apprehending realities closed to the categories of the intellect.

Rumi also agrees with Al-Ghazali that this status comes only through mystical experience and it is different from any other experience:

> Then again, besides the reason and soul of the
> [ordinary] man,
> There is another soul [life] in the prophet and
> the saint.
> The spirit of revelation is more hidden than
> reason itself
> Because it belongs to the unseen on the other
> side [of reason].[10]
> The inspiration of God is not [like] astrology
> or geomancy or dreams—and God best knoweth
> what is right.
> The Sufis in explaining their doctrine call it
> [the divine inspiration] the inspiration of
> the heart, in order to disguise [its real
> nature] from the vulgar.
> Take it to be the inspiration of the heart, for
> it [the heart] is the place where He is seen:
> How should there be error when the heart
> is aware of Him?

---

[9] Al-Ghazali, Ihy al Ulum, quoted by Khalifa, *Metaphysics of Rumi*, pp. 102–3.
[10] Rumi, *Masnavi*, vol. 3 (Teheran Press, 1924), p. 68.

Rumi's boldness and courage are worth admiring. He frankly admits that revelation of the heart, a term invented by the Sufis, is not in essence very different from the revelation of the prophets. He furthermore defines the *heart* as the receiver of Divine Realities. No evil comes to us from the outside and everything good or bad comes from our hearts:

When you are ready, I need not say anything any more. The Holy Ghost shall talk to you without my interference.
The voice coming to your ears is not yours or mine or anybody else. It is like a dream which you hear things from your own self and think that somebody else said it to you.[11]

In another place, Rumi explains that the source of revelation is eternal spirit of man himself:

The parrot whose voice comes from the Divine revelation and whose beginning pre-dates your existence is hidden within you. You have seen the reflection of this parrot upon many things [in this phenomenal world].[12]

Sufis believe that revelation is not a monopoly of a few men whom we call prophets. They even contend that God made the honeybee the recipient of revelation by inspiring him how to suck nectar from different flowers and build and manage his honeycomb. Rumi tells us further that all arts, sciences, and poetry have their origin in a flash of inspiration, though later on experience improves them.

The spiritual ear becomes the recipient of
revelations.
What is this revelation but the faculty hidden
from sense-perception.
The spiritual ear and eye are different from
this sense-perception.
The ears of intellect and the eyes of assumption
are beggars before this hidden power.[13]

---

[11] Ibid., vol. 5, v. 1290–1301.
[12] Ibid., vol. 1, v. 1717–18.
[13] Ibid., v. 1461–62.

Since Rumi believed in the potentialities for divine values of every human soul, he boldly denied the finality of prophethood. It is surprising that his assumption maintaining that every individual has ability not only to become a saint but to become a prophet was ignored by the theologians:

> Try to be of service to your community in order
> to become a prophet in a nation.
> All the sciences and arts begin with revelations,
> later intellect and experience improves them.[14]

This new doctrine of Sufis identifying the divine with human souls brought death to Hallaj, it is a mystery why the idea of claiming sainthood and prophethood saved Rumi from excommunication.

In his elaboration of this doctrine, Rumi stands on a hill all by himself. For him there is no fundamental difference between sainthood and prophethood, because both represent a stage of development realizable by every individual:

> The story of Moses has become a chain of historical events which happened in ancient times. Moses' story serves as a mask, it is the light of Moses and his revelation that you are seeking, O good man.

> Moses and Pharaoh are two forces hidden inside you. Thou must seek these two adversaries in your heart.[15]

In this statement, Rumi is indicating that the story of Moses is more than a historical event, but a drama of an eternal play enacted in every human soul.

What is the Sufis' conception of this ideal man:

> The man who abandons "self" becomes the best of beings and the great one among them. He has identified himself with Truth and abandoned his "self". In reality he has earned eternal life. At this stage all faculties are under his control and all bodies are under his command. He who places himself

---

14 Ibid., vol. 5, v. 469, and vol. 4, v. 1296–97.
15 Ibid., vol. 3, v. 1251, 1253.

under the protection of God is not a slave but a free and favorite friend.

In his *Divan Shams*, Rumi calls the ideal man a man of God and describes him in the following words:

> The man of God is drunken without wine,
> The man of God is full without meat.
> The man of God is distraught and bewildered,
> The man of God has no food or sleep.
> The man of God is a king beneath darvish-cloak,
> The man of God is a treasure in a ruin
> The man of God is not of air and earth,
> The man of God is not of fire and water.
> The man of God is a boundless sea,
> The man of God rains pearls without cloud.
> The man of God hath hundred moons and skies,
> The man of God hath hundred suns.
> The man of God is made wise by God,
> The man of God is learned not by book.
> The man of God is beyond infidelity and fidelity,
> The man of God is beyond right and wrong.
> The man of God was elect before his creation,
> The man of God is gloriously received.
> The man of God is hidden, Oh Shamsi Din,
> The man of God do thou seek and find.[16]

According to the Sufis, it is possible for every individual to become an ideal man. Any man or woman who reaches this stage is covered with the mantle of the divinity and it is indifferent whether one calls him or her a saint or a prophet.

To summarize Sufi ideas of an ideal man:

• He is in immediate touch with God; neither prophet nor angels intervene between the two.

• He is one with God, and with this unity no plurality exists;

• He can work miracles that do not mean moving the mountains but turning hatred and bitterness into love and happiness.

---

[16] Rumi, *Divan Sham*, Tabriz, translated by Nicholson (Cambridge: University Press, 1898), pp. 28–30.

• He is identical with Lago or the universal reason that creates and governs the universe.

• He is the final cause of creation; he is the last of creation in point of time but existed before creation as an idea.

• He is the embodiment of universal reason and is identified with universal soul.

There is always a possibility of having an ideal man. Every age has seen many of them. Ideal man is dead to himself, but he lives in God and his purpose is to serve his fellow men. No words can explain the nature of this union of God and man, and no age or land can exist without the ideal man. In every era a saint arises, and this experience will continue until the day of Judgment.

"The saint, then is the living leader [Imam] who appears in every age regardless of whether he is the descendant of Ali or Umar."

# 6

## The Sources of Sufi Ideas of Universalism and Human Rights

I have raised Cyrus up in righteousness, and I will direct all his ways; he shall build my city, and shall let go my captives, not for price nor reward, said the Lord of the hosts.

Isaiah

Persian Sufi poets seek unity of man, universalism, and tolerance as the basis of faith.

The question is often asked "Where are the sources of these tolerant and humane ideas?" The answer could be found in the ancient culture of Iran. Persians were Aryan in their language, but their culture, like their empire, was universal. They served historically as conveyors and as the melting pot of different civilizations that became a part of their empire.

Cyrus the Great (b. 589 B.C.) was the first enlightened king to forge the heterogeneous nations he had conquered into a universal empire through the exercise of tolerance, mutual respect, and cultural and religious freedom. It was a common custom, before and after the appearance of Cyrus on the surface of world history, for kings and generals to take the people of a conquered country captive and make them slaves. They employed them, to some extent, as personal household servants, but more generally as agricultural laborers to till the land. Cyrus prohibited the killing or enslaving of the prisoners. He decreed that all religions should be tolerated. Whenever he conquered a country he proclaimed that all the slaves should be set free and that the exiles and captive people should return to their respective lands and be ruled by a native governor of their own choice.

When Cyrus conquered Babylon in 538 B.C., he found a large number of Jews in captivity. An account of the captivity of the Jews in Babylon is given in the closing chapters of the Second Book of Chronicles, though many of the events are more fully detailed in the Book of Jeremiah. Nebuchadnezzar, the King of Babylon, made repeated incursions into the land of Judea, sometimes carrying away the reigning monarch, on occasions deposing him and appointing another sovereign in his stead, often assessing taxes and tribute upon the whole nation, and at times plundering the city and carrying away not only all gold and silver but all the strong-bodied men and women. King Zedekiah was the last of the oppressed and unhappy line of Jewish kings. Many inhabitants of Judea were carried away by the Babylonians, and for two generations remained in miserable bondage in Babylon. Some of them were employed as agricultural laborers in the rural districts of Babylon; others remained in the city and were engaged in servile labors there. The Prophet Daniel lived in the palaces and in the service of the King of Babylon. He was summoned to Belshazzar's feast on the night when Cyrus forced his way into the city to interpret the mysterious writing on the wall, by which the fall of the Babylonian monarchy was announced in so terrible a manner.

One year after Cyrus had conquered Babylon, he issued an edict authorizing the Jews to return to Jerusalem, and to rebuild the city and the temple. The Prophet Ezra, referring to this royal magnanimity states:

Now in the first year of Cyrus, King of Persia, so that the word of the Lord spoken through Jeremiah might be fulfilled the Lord stirred up the heart of Cyrus, King of Persia; and he issued a proclamation throughout the kingdom, both by word of mouth and in writing to this effect: "This is the word of Cyrus, King of Persia; the Lord God of heaven has given me all the kingdoms of the earth, and he himself has charged me to build Him a House at Jerusalem in Judah. To every man of His people now amongst you I say, God be with him, and let him go up to Jerusalem in Judah, and rebuild the House of the Lord, whose city is Jerusalem. And every remaining Jew, wherever he may be living, may claim aid from his neighbors in that place, silver and gold, goods and cattle, in addition to the voluntary offerings for the House of God in Jerusalem."

Thereupon, the heads of families of Judah and Benjamin, and the priests and the Levites, answered the summons, all whom God had moved to go up to rebuild the House of the Lord in Jerusalem. Their neighbors all assisted them with gifts of every kind, silver, and gold, goods and cattle and valuable gifts in abundance, in addition to any voluntary service. Moreover, Cyrus, King of Persia, brought forth the vessels of the house of the Lord which Nebuchadnezzar had removed from Jerusalem and placed in the Temple of his God; and he handed them over into the charge of Mithredath the Treasurer, who made an inventory of them for Sheshbazzar the Ruler of Judah. . . . The vessels of gold and silver amounted in all to five thousand four hundred; and Sheshbazzar took them all up to Jerusalem, when the exiles were brought back from Babylon.[1]

Ezra then points out that by the order from the King of Persia they paid money for the masons, carpenters, food, drink, and oil for Sidonians and Tyrians who worked on the rebuilding of Jerusalem. When others wanted to help, the heads of the Jewish families answered, "The House we are building for our God is our concern . . . as his majesty Cyrus King of Persia commanded us."[2]

Later on, according to Ezra, Darius the Great, Cyrus's successor, issued an order to the governors of the province Beyond-Euphrates

"to leave the governor of the Jews and their elders free to rebuild this House of God . . . the expenses are to be defrayed in full from the royal funds accruing from the taxes of the province Beyond-Euphrates, so that the work may not be

---

[1] Ezra 1:1–11.
[2] Ezra 11:4–5.

brought to a standstill. And let them have daily without fail whatever they want, young bulls, rams, or lambs as whole-offering for the God of heaven, or wheat, salt, wine, or oil, as the priests in Jerusalem demand, so that they may offer soothing sacrifices to the God of heaven, and pray for the life of the King and his sons. Furthermore, I decree that, if any man tampers with this edict, a beam shall be pulled out of his house and he shall be fastened erect to it and flogged; and in addition his house shall be forfeit . . . I, Darius, have issued a decree; it is to be carried out to the letter.[3]

"Let the work of this House of God alone; let the governor of the Jews and the elders of the Jews build this House of God in his place. Moreover, I make a decree what ye shall do to the elders of these Jews for the building of this House of God: that of the king's good, even of the tribute beyond the river, forthwith expenses be given unto these men, that they be not hindered.

"And the God that hath caused his name to dwell there destroy all kings and people, that shall put to their hand to alter and to destroy this House of God which is at Jerusalem. I Darius have made a decree; let it be done with speed."

And the elders of the Jews builded, and they prospered. . . . And they builded, and finished it, according to the commandment of the God of Israel, and according to the commandment of Cyrus, and Darius, and Artaxerxes, Kings of Persia.[4]

Ezra, the author of this story, was a scribe at the court of the Persian King Artaxerxes in Susa. When the king heard of the feud among the Jewish families and famine and hardship in Jerusalem, some thirty years after their return, he ordered Ezra to organize a second Zionade, which proved successful beyond all expectations.

The following is the context of the royal letter that the King of Persia had given to Ezra:

Artaxerxes, king of kings, unto Ezra the priest, the scribe of the Law of the God of heaven, and so forth. And now I make a decree, that all they of the people of Israel, and their

---

[3] Ezra 6:6–13.
[4] Ezra 6.

priests and the Levites, in my realm, that are minded of their own free will to go with thee to Jerusalem, go. For as much as thou art sent of the king and his seven counsellors, to inquire concerning Judah and Jerusalem, according to the law of thy God which is in thy hand; and to carry the silver and gold, which the king and his counsellors have freely offered unto the God of Israel, whose habitation is in Jerusalem, and all the silver and gold that thou shalt find in all the province of Babylon, with the freewill-offering of the people, and of the priests, offering willingly for the house of their God which is in Jerusalem; therefore thou shalt with all diligence buy with this money bullocks, rams, lambs, with their meal-offerings and their drink-offerings, and shalt offer them upon the altar of the house of your God which is in Jerusalem. And whatsoever shall seem good to thee and to thy brethren to do with the rest of the silver and the gold, that do ye after the will of your God. And the vessels that are given thee for the service of the House of thy God, deliver thou before the God of Jerusalem. And whatsoever shall seem good to thee and to thy brethren to do with the rest of the silver and the gold, that do ye after the will of your God. And the vessels that are given thee for the service of the House of thy God, deliver thou before the God of Jerusalem. And whatsoever more shall be needful for the House of thy God, which thou shalt have occasion to bestow, bestow it out of the king's treasure-house. And I, even I Artaxerxes the king, do make a decree to all the treasurers that are beyond the River, that whatsoever Ezra the priest, the scribe of the Law of the God of heaven, shall require of you, it be done with all diligence, unto a hundred talents of silver, and to a hundred measures of wheat, and to a hundred baths of wine, and to a hundred baths of oil, and salt without prescribing how much.

Whatsoever is commanded by the God of heaven, let it be done exactly for the House of the God of heaven; for why should there be wrath against the realm of the king and his sons? Also we announce to you, that touching any of the priests and Levites, the singers, porters, Nethinim, or servants of this House of God, it shall not be lawful to impose tribute, impost, or toll upon them. And thou, Ezra, after the wisdom of thy God that is in thy hand, appoint magistrates and judges, who may judge all the people that are beyond the River, all such as know the laws of thy God; and teach ye him that knoweth them not. And whatsoever will not do the law of thy God, and the law of the king, let judgment be executed upon him with all diligence, whether it be unto death, or to banishment, or to confiscation of goods, or to imprisonment.

Blessed be the Lord, the God of our fathers, who hath put such a thing as this in the king's heart, to beautify the House of the Lord which is in Jerusalem; and hath extended mercy unto me before the king, and his counsellors, and before all the king's mighty princes. And I was strengthened according to the hand of the Lord my God upon me, and I gathered together out of Israel chief men to go up with me.

Later on, King Artaxerxes dispatched Nehemiah, his cup-bearer, to Jerusalem. The team of Ezra and Nehemiah, with the King's financial and military help, fortified Jerusalem and protected Jews from the attacks of hostile neighbors. Referring to this story, Nehemiah states:

When I was in Susa, the capital city [of Persia] it happened that one of my brothers arrived . . . from Judah; I asked about Jerusalem and about the Jews. . . . They told me that those still remaining in the province who had survived the captivity were facing great trouble and reproach, the wall of Jerusalem was broken down and the gates had been destroyed by fire. When I heard this news, I sat down and wept. . . .

Now at this time I was the King's cup-bearer and one day, in the month Nisan, in the twentieth year of King Artaxerxes, when his wine was ready, I took it up and handed it to the King, and I stood before him I was feeling very unhappy. He said to me, "Why do you look so unhappy?" . . . I answered, "If it please your majesty, and if I enjoy your favor, I beg you to send me to Judah, to the city where my forefathers are buried, so that I may rebuild it." The King with the queen consort sitting next to him, asked me, "How long will the journey last and when will you return?" Then the King approved the request and let me go and I told him how long I should be. Then I said to the King, "If it please your majesty, let letters be given me for the governors in the province of Beyond-Euphrates with orders to grant me all the help I need for my journey to Judah. Let me have also a letter for Asaph, the keeper of your royal forests, instructing him to supply me with timber to make beams for the gates of the citadel, which adjoins the palace, and for the city wall, and for the palace which I shall occupy." The King granted my requests, for the gracious hand of my God was upon me. I came in due course to the governors in the province of Beyond-Euphrates and presented them the King's letters; the King had given me an escort of army officers with cavalry.

Nehemiah found the situation in Jerusalem intolerable:

Some complained that they were giving their sons and daughters as pledges for food to keep themselves alive; others that they were mortgaging their fields, vineyards and houses to buy corn in the famine; others that they were borrowing money on their fields and vineyards to pay taxes.

People were selling their children and many boys and girls had already been enslaved by the rich Jews in Jerusalem.

When Nehemiah saw the tragic and tormenting condition of the common people of Judea, he severely rebuked the rich leaders of the Jewish community, saying:

As far as we have been able, we have bought back our fellow Jews who had been sold to other nations, but you are now selling your own fellow countrymen, and they will have to be bought back by us.

It was at this time that Artaxerxes appointed Nehemiah governor and leader of Judea. Since he enjoyed both the military and the financial support of the King of Persia, Nehemiah was able to introduce a number of reforms. His twelve-year rule brought Judea success and prosperity beyond expectation.

The magnanimity of Cyrus and his successors brought praise and prayers from another leader of Judea, Isaiah, who applauds him as a messiah, destined to deliver his people from bondage.

When Cyrus was campaigning against Croesus of Lydia, Isaiah cautiously refers to Cyrus as the man of the north:

I, God the first, and unto the future I am. I raised up him of the north and him of the East; they shall be called by my name, let the rulers come; and as the potter his clay, as the potter tramples his clay, so shall you be trampled.

Later Isaiah dares to be much more explicit:

Thus saith the Lord, thy liberator and he that formed thee from the womb; I am the Lord who maketh all things; I spread forth the heavens alone, and made fast the earth. Who else shall scatter the signs of the mediums and the soothsayers, turning cunning men back and making their counsel folly? . . . He that saith to Jerusalem, thou shalt be inhabited, and to the cities of Edam, ye shalt be built; and he will restore her desolate places; who saith to the deep, "Be dry", and I will dry up thy springs; who biddeth Cyrus be wise, and he shall perform all my pleasure; who saith to Jerusalem, thou shalt be built, and I lay the foundations of my holy house.

Thus saith the Lord unto Cyrus, my Anointed, whose right hand I have grasped, that the nation shall obey Him, and I will break the strength of Kings; I will go before thee and level mountains; I will shatter gates of bronze, and smash bars of iron, and will give thee the hidden treasures of darkness; I will open to thee the unseen places; that thou mayest know that I am the Lord, the God who called thee by thy name, the God of Israel.

Later on in the same chapter, Isaiah heaps more praise on Cyrus the Great:

I form the light, and create darkness: I make peace, and create evil: I, the Lord, do all things.

Drop down, ye heaven, from above, and let the skies pour down righteousness: let the earth open, and let them bring forth salvation, and let righteousness spring up together; I the Lord have created it.

I have raised him [Cyrus] up in righteousness, and I will direct all his ways; he shall build my city, and shall let go my captives, not for price nor reward, saith the Lord of the hosts.

Thus saith the Lord, the labour of Egypt, and merchandise,

of Ethiopia and of the Saboan, men of stature, shall come over unto thee, and they shall be thine; they shall come after thee; in chains they shall come over, and they shall fall down unto thee, they shall make supplications unto thee saying, surely God is in thee; and there is none else.[5]

Many historians are astonished by the way that Isaiah has addressed Cyrus twice as "My anointed," which in Hebrew is "My Messiah," and in Latin *Christo Meo* (as in the Greek). This was possibly shocking to many Jews that their messiah should be an Aryan king. "Striking, too is the extent to which the prophet used words here and elsewhere, which might be expected to appeal to Persians. The repeated reference to 'justice' and 'the just' or 'the Righteous One', reminds us of the Persian word sita, 'the right', frequent in their royal inscriptions and a common element in Persian names."

Isaiah concludes his address to Cyrus by stating:

For the sake of Jacob my servant and Israel my chosen
I have called you by name and given you your title, though
you have not known me. So that men from the rising and
the setting sun may know that there is none but I:

I am the Lord, there is no other,
I make the light, I create darkness,
Author alike of prosperity and trouble.
I, the Lord, do all these things.

Rain righteousness, you heavens,
    let the skies above pour down;
That it may bear the fruit of salvation
    with righteousness in blossom at its side.
All this I, the Lord, have created.

In the above address, the words *light, darkness,* and *righteousness* point very strongly to the language used at the time of Cyrus in Iran. They came from the attributes of Ahura-Mazda, who is light and righteous, and Ahriman, which stands for "darkness" and "evil." This address and other writings of Isaiah show his

---

[5] Isaiah 40–55.

confidence in Cyrus and the belief that here was another Messiah permitting not only the exiled Jews to return to Jerusalem, but ready to rebuild the Temple and to send back all the sacred vessels taken therefrom, which had been preserved in Babylonian temple treasuries.

The severity and gloom of the previous pronouncements of Isaiah are now replaced by a promise of future joy and happiness and rejuvenation. The Divine Spirit manifested by Cyrus will shine over Jerusalem and the rising generations will flock together, and all of them return to Jerusalem. Cyrus's generosity will lavish the riches and wealth of the nations upon them. For the present all was joy, because Cyrus would look after the interests of Israel as a shepherd looks after his flock:

Arise, Jerusalem,
Rise clothed in light; your light has come
    and the glory of the Lord shines over you.
For, though darkness covers the earth
    and dark night the nations,
The Lord shall shine upon you
And over you shall his glory appear;
    and the nations shall march towards your light
    and their Kings to your sunrise.
Lift up your eyes and look all around;
They flock together, all of them, and come to you;
Your sons also shall come from afar,
Your daughters walking beside them leading the way.
Then shall you see, and shine with Joy,
Then your heart shall thrill with pride:
The riches of the sea shall be lavished upon you
    and you shall possess the wealth of nations.[6]

Of the coming fate of Babylon, Isaiah speaks with vindictive harshness:

Down! Sit in the dust, virgin daughter of Babylon! . . . Never more shall it be thine to be called soft and luxurious. Take the queen, grind flour, take off thy veil.

[6] A. R. Burn, *Persia and the Greeks* (London: Edward Arnold, 1962), pp. 54–58.

The author of the famous Psalm 137 was more embittered than Isaiah:

> O daughter of Babylon, that art to be destroyed,
> Happy shall he be that rewardeth thee as thou
>     hast served us:
> Happy shall he be that taketh thy little ones
>     and dashed them upon the stone.

But these horrible wishes were never fulfilled. Cyrus had no intention of destroying the city or enslaving the people. He respected the Babylonian tradition, religion, and gods. In the spring of 538 his son Cambyses was installed as king of Babylon and went through the historic New Year ritual. He did homage to Bel and Nebo; Cyrus was never a dogmatic monotheist. "The Verse Account" of Nabonidus tells the story of his reign in a hostile manner, and celebrates Cyrus as a liberator almost as enthusiastically as the "second Isaiah;" especially his release of the gods whom Nabonidus had concentrated in Babylon, to return with joy to their homes. The preserved part of the text ends:

> To inhabitants of Babylon a heart is given;
> They are like prisoners when the prisons are
>     opened;
> Liberty is restored to those who were surrounded
>     by oppression;
> All rejoice to look upon him as King.[7]

In the cuneiform text on the Cyrus Cylinder, a similar picture is given:

> Nabonidus was heretical; he changed the details of worship
> the way also an oppressor, exhausting the people with forced
> labor; he is to be given no credit for his works on the restoration
> of temples; only the labor is emphasized. But Bel-Marduk
> cast his eye over all countries, seeking for a righteous ruler
> . . . . Then he called by name Cyrus, King of Anshan, and
> pronounced him ruler of lands. And Cyrus treated justly the

---

[7] Ibid., pp. 56–58.

"black-headed" people whom Marduk had made him to conquer.[8]

In this description, the emphasis is placed on the heretical behavior of Nabonidus, the restoration of the right worship of God by Cyrus, the peaceful, disciplined character of occupation, and the magnanimity of the Iranians who occupied Babylon.

When in 538 B.C. Cyrus entered Babylon the world was already an old world. But he was the first king to establish a universal empire, from Ionia to India, built up from diverse peoples, based on an enlightened policy of liberality, understanding, and tolerance and freedom for all the races, religions, and local systems.

As the founder of this universal monarchy, Cyrus was not only the greatest conqueror, but a magnanimous reformer who respected the rights of minorities and encouraged freedom of worship. In eleven years, Cyrus thrusted on one side into the heart of India, and on the other side conquered Babylon, Lydia, Media, and all the adjacent territories as far as the Mediterranean Sea Thus the first and the greatest universal empire came into being. For centuries historians have asked "Why did Cyrus achieve such a sweeping success?" The answers have ranged from the youthful energies of Cyrus and his new army to the crisis of the ancient empires, their wars, their corruption and decadence.

Unfortunately, both the historians and propagandists have neglected to mention Cyrus's highest qualities, applauded by so many prophets and teachers of the Old Testament and Greek historians. It is certain, from these documents, that such an extensive empire consisting of peoples and cultures extremely different from one another could not have survived without justice and a political formula in which the old cultures and the new system could be reconciled. Consequently, resistance and conflict changed into cooperation, concord, and confederation. As a result, Cyrus and his successors' contributions paved the way for a more compassionate and tolerant world. Everywhere they encouraged respect for local tradition, individual rights to worship, compassion for the captives, consideration and care for the weak.

---

[8] Ibid.

Moreover, in an age when every small group called themselves the chosen people or the selects, when every conqueror either killed or enslaved the conquered, when cruelty, callousness, and atrocities were the order of the day, Cyrus and his successors present themselves as the champions of various traditions, local customs, and different religions. Some historians attribute this respect for human rights to propaganda and expediency. But, one should ask, propaganda for what? The Persian kings were not elected heads of the state to depend on the votes of Babylonians, Jews, or Medians. They had no fear of the United Nations or human rights commission. There were no dissidents, no labor unions, and no opposition party. They defied their own people (Persians), who considered themselves better than the other races. They disputed Babylonians who considered Jews their slaves. They disagreed with Jews and Medians who considered their gods the only gods. They asserted that all gods should be respected because each man and woman creates his own god in his or her own image. They introduced ideas and principles that even today are beyond the reach of many nations. The assertion of the moral principle, the elevation of tolerance to a system, the rights of minorities, compassion and consideration of the weak, the aim at co-existence beyond the points established even today, "all bear witness to an indubitably high ethical level and a concrete liberality, and determine the advance of practical action along the lines indicated by the theoretical premises."[9]

There are forty-two references, stories, and documents concerning the outstanding achievements of Cyrus, Darius, and Artaxerxes, kings of Persia, in the books of Isaiah, Daniel, Ezra, and Nehemiah. They all bear witness to greatness, tolerance, magnanimity, and humanity of these men in an age of cruelty and brutality. They also show the profound appreciation of the prophets for their unprecedented generosity:

So this Daniel prospered in the reign of Cyrus the Persian.[10]
Know therefore and discern, that from the going forth of the word to restore and to build Jerusalem unto one anointed,

---

[9] S. Moscati, *The Face of the Ancient Middle East* (New York: Anchor Books, 1962), pp. 287–88.
[10] Daniel 6:29.

a prince, shall be seven weeks; and for threescore and two weeks it shall be built again.[11]

In the third year of Cyrus King of Persia a word was revealed unto David.

Now in the first year of Cyrus, King of Persia, that the word of the Lord by the mouth of Jeremiah might be accomplished, the Lord stirred up the spirit of Cyrus King of Persia, that he made a proclamation throughout his kingdom.[12]

Ye have nothing to do with us to build a house unto our God; but we ourselves together will build unto the Lord, the God of Israel, as King Cyrus, the King of Persia hath commanded us.

But in the first year of Cyrus King of Babylon, Cyrus the King made a decree to build this House of God.[13]

And they builded and finished it, according to the commandment of the God of Israel, and according to the decree of Cyrus and Darius and Artaxerxes King of Persia.[14]

> I have commanded my consecrated ones,
> Yea, I have called my mighty ones for my anger
> Even my proudly exalting ones.
>
> A grievous vision is declared unto me:
> The treacherous dealer dealeth treacherously,
>     and the spoiler spoileth.
> Go up O Elam! Besiege O Media!
> All the sighing thereof have I made to cease.[15]

When Cyrus conquered Elam and Media and the news of his generosity, compassion, and humane treatment of the conquered nations reached Babylon, Isaiah openly praised Cyrus:[16]

---

11 Daniel 9:25.
12 Ezra 1:1.
13 Ezra 5:13.
14 Ezra 6:14.
15 Isaiah 13:3, referring to the march of Cyrus's forces on Babylon.
16 Isaiah's prophecy on the capture of Babylon by Cyrus, King of Elam and Media.

Who hath raised one from the East,
And whose steps victory attendeth?
He giveth nations before him,
And maketh him to rule over kings;
His sword marketh them as the dust,
His bow as the driven stubble.[17]

I have roused up one from the north, and
    he is come,
From the rising of the sun one that calleth
    upon my name;
And he shall come upon rulers as upon mortar,
And as the potter treadeth clay.[18]

Isaiah describes Cyrus as "the ideal servant of God, an elect, quiet, and unobtrusive man whose spiritual influence would spread throughout the world." Isaiah then in the name of God declares: "I have put my spirit upon him. He shall make the right to go forth to the nations. . . . He shall make the right to go forth according to the truth."

Furthermore, Isaiah describes the rise of Cyrus and his conquest in the following words:

Assemble yourselves, all ye, and hear;
Which among them hath declared these things?
He whom the Lord loveth shall perform his
    pleasure on Babylon,
And show his arm on the Chaldeans.[19]

Daniel, referring to the contribution of Persians to freedom and justice for the Jews, states:

And as for me, in the first year of Darius the Mede,
I stood up to be a supporter and a stronghold unto
    him,
And now will I declare unto the truth, Behold, there
    shall stand up yet three kings in Persia;
    and the fourth shall be far richer than they all;

---

[17] Isaiah  41:2.
[18] Isaiah  4:28.
[19] Isaiah  48:14.

and when he is waxed strong through his riches,
He shall stir up all against the realm of Greece.[20]

Ezra, in his account of the rebuilding of the temple at the time of Darius, states that Tattenai, the governor of the land beyond the river Tigris, reported to Darius that the Jews were fortifying the city of Jerusalem. When he tried to stop them they declared that Cyrus, the king of Persia, in the first year of the capture of Babylon "decreed to build this House of the Lord. Then Darius, the king made a decree, and search was made in the house of the archives, where the treasures were laid up in Babylon."

Then Darius ordered the governor of the area beyond the Tigris River[21] "to let the work of this House of God alone; let the governor of the Jews and the elders of the Jews build this House of God in its place. Moreover, I make a decree concerning what ye shall do to these elders of the Jews for the building of this House of God, that of the King's goods, even of the tribute beyond the river, expenses be given with all diligence unto these men, that they be not hindered."

Nehemiah, in his description of the rebuilding of the temple at the time of King Artaxerxes states:

For there was a commandment from the king concerning them and a sure ordinance concerning the singers, as every day required. And Pethahiah, the son of Meshazabel, of the Children of Zerah the son of Judah, was at the King's hand in all matters concerning the people.[22]

While Nehemiah, Ezra, and Isaiah claim that God of Judah anointed Cyrus to save the Jews from bondage and rebuild the Temple, the Babylonian inscription asserts that Marduk, the Lord protector of Babylon, chose Cyrus and sent him to restore justice and faith in Babylon:

Marduk scanned and looked through all the countries, seeking a righteous ruler willing to lead him in the annual procession.

---

20 Daniel 11:1 and 2.
21 Ezra 6:8–15.
22 Nehemiah 11:26.

He uttered the name of Cyrus, King of Anshan, declaring him ruler of all the world. Marduk, the great lord, protector of his people, beheld with joy Cyrus' good deeds and his upright heart, and bade him march against his city Babylon. He made him set out on the road to Babylon, going at his side, as a true friend. His huge army, its number, like that of the waters of a river, could not be counted, marched on with their weapons packed away. Without any battle, Marduk brought them into his town of Babylon, sparing it from calamity. He delivered into Cyrus' hands Nobonidus, the King, who did not worship him. All the inhabitants of Babylon as well as the entire land of Sumer and Akkad, princes and governors included, bowed to Cyrus and kissed his feet, jubilant and with shining faces because he had received the Kingship. Happily they greeted him as the master by whose help they had come back to life out of death and had been spared disaster, and they worshipped his very name.[23]

The proclamation of Cyrus to the Babylonians was issued in their own language. It represents Cyrus's philosophy and his way of thinking. After making it clear that he was the legitimate successor of the former rulers of Babylon, he cites the faults and the heresies of Nabu-naid and his sin against Marduk, the king of the gods. He also reminds people of Babylon and other cities that under the former ruler and his priests they were given rituals unbefitting them; that their former ruler daily manifested enmity to Marduk's city; all Marduk's people be brought to the ruin through servitude without rest.

Because of their complaints, the lord of the gods became furiously angry with them and abandoned their country. The gods who dwelt among them left their homes in wrath because strange gods had been brought into Babylon. But soon Marduk repented and granted mercy to all the dwelling places which had become ruinous and to the people of Sumer and Akkad who were like corpses.

Later on, Cyrus states that

when I made my gracious entry into Babylon, with rejoicing

---

[23] Moscati, *Ancient Middle East*, p. 288.

and pleasure I took up my lordly residence in the royal palace. Marduk, the great lord, turned the noble race of the Babylonians towards me. I gave daily care to his worship. My numerous troops marched peacefully into Babylon. In all Sumer and Akkad I permitted no unfriendly treatment. The dishonoring yoke was removed from Him. Their fallen dwellings I restored; I cleared out the ruins.

Marduk, the great lord, rejoiced in my pious deeds, and graciously blessed me, Cyrus, the King who worships him, and Cambyses, my own son, and all my soldiers, while we, in sincerity and with joy praised his exalted godhead. All the kings dwelling in palaces of all the quarters of the earth, from the upper to the lower sea, and all the kings of the Amorite country who dwelt in tents [the Arabs] brought me their heavy gifts and in Babylon kissed my feet.

Then Cyrus tells how

Nabu-naid was an exceedingly wicked monarch; righteousness and justice never accompanied him. The weak he smote by the sword. He blocked the road to the merchants. The peasant was deprived of his plow land; never he raised the Harvest shout of rejoicing. The irrigation system was allowed to fall into neglect. Prominent men were imprisoned. The citizen assembly was disturbed, their countenances were changed; they did walk in the open place. The city did not see pleasure. He spoke a word against the divine commands and uttered impiety. By his own hands, the divine symbols were torn down from the sacred place.[24]

Cyrus, to everybody's surprise, at the conclusion of the proclamation declared peace and amnesty for all. He slaughtered a lamb outside the temple. He increased the incense for God's offering. He restored every sanctuary. The great New Year's feast abandoned by Nabu-naid was re-established.[25]

While still residing in Babylon, Cyrus received homage from the king of Syria, rulers of Phoenicia, and Nobatean. This meant

---

[24] A. T. Olmstead, *History of the Persian Empire* (Chicago: University of Chicago Press, 1948), pp. 55–57.

[25] Ibid., p. 58.

that Cyrus's empire at this time extended from Indus to the Mediterranean.

No historian has been ever able to express the personality, philosophy, and the ideas of Cyrus better than his own words in the following inscription:

> I am Cyrus, King of the world, the great King, the legitimate King, King of Babylon, King of Sumer and Akkad, King of the corners of the earth (son of Cyrus the son of Cambyses the son of Peispes) of a family which has always exercised kingship; whose rule Bel and Nebo love. Cyrus commends himself to the gods, together with Cambyses my son, the offspring of my loins and his army. "All the kings of the whole world, from the upper to the lower sea, those who sit in throne-rooms, those who live in other, . . . all the kings of the world dwelling in tents [the Median and Kedar of the Hebrew poet] brought their heavy tribute and kissed my feet. And Cyrus restored sanctuaries and houses [war damage] and gave peace to Babylon."[26]

"I am Cyrus, King of the world." Such is the proud declaration that, after the lapse of twenty-five centuries, from the tomb of the noble Persian king, still commands our respect and homage. Out of the realm of myth, fable, and negligence, Cyrus's noble figure emerges and history discovers enough about him so that his title of "the great" stands unquestioned. Media surrendered to him, Croesus, with all his treasure, went down before him, great Babylon welcomed him with open arms, and Isaiah sang his praise as the Messiah and deliverer of his people, and as the right hand of God destined to save the people of Israel.

"Great as are his records as the conqueror, as warrior, and as a prince, his empire could not have survived without a political theory of its own and a system in which the old and new could be reconciled, the resistances and conflicts diminished, and the tendencies to harmony, cooperation, and union fostered and strengthened." Indeed, Cyrus's greatest achievement is precisely in this direction. Everywhere he respects local traditions and

---

[26] Moscati, *Ancient Middle East*, p. 294.

adapts himself to them. "Moreover, with his distinctive view of history he presents himself as the legitimate successor to the local dynasties, which have been found wanting because of the fault of their representatives; he takes over existing institutions without modification; he honors the gods of other peoples and makes them his own."[27]

Thus, in the sixth century B.C., Cyrus of Persia not only established a universal Empire but as an avant-garde Sufi, set examples for future rulers and leaders concerning respect for human rights, freedom of religion, and dissent.

-------

The Sufi philosophy was also influenced by the ideas and teachings of Zoroaster.

"The factor which had the greatest effect in shaping Iranian civilization, and its becoming a cultural as well as a distinctive political entity for more than two thousand years," according to *Enciclopedia Cattolica*, "is certainly the influence of religion. For whereas the Iranian tribes of the plateau, who made the religion of Zoroaster their own, became an historical people, capable of establishing powers and a civilization on the fringe of the Greco-Roman-world, the other tribes of Asia, who remained aloof from that religion, were lost to view in the sea of nomadic peoples to which the ancient world gave the collective name of Scythians. Be it observed, moreover, that the self-assertion of Iranian civilization, especially on the cultural level, appears in its various developments to have a close connection with the affirmation of those religious values."[28]

These observations clearly express the importance of the religion of Zoroaster on Cyrus, Darius, and the people of the Plateau of Iran. This is confirmed by the twenty-five centuries of history in which Zoroastrianism has survived the fall of many dynasties and half a dozen invasions. The impact of Zoroastrianism is not limited to Iran and Sufi poetry, it extends to the whole of ancient and modern world. It forms a parallel to events in Palestine, for it asserts a monotheistic creed with moral foundation. The differ-

-------

27 Ibid., p. 289.
28 A. Pagliaro, *Enciclopedia Cattolica*, vol. 9 (Citta del Vaticano: 1952), col. 1206.

ence between the two religions is profound: In Israel faith and politics were fused into an indissoluble unity: in Iran they were distinct and different; in old Judah monotheism had a mainly emotional basis; in Iran the intellectual outlook prevailed, and it would be difficult to isolate this—though it is not easy to be more precise—from the behavior and characteristics of the Indo-European tribes that are its bearers; finally in Palestine, monotheism grew more and more absolute, where in Iran it is attenuated as time passes. "Yet in spite of these differences, and in spite of the even more obvious ones arising from the profound dissimilarity of the environment and other conditions, the two religions are linked by one essential bond: in both cases a faith breaks away into independence, and so constitutes a community—we would say, a Church independent of political conditions."[29]

Zoroaster (Zartusht in Persian) began his mission in the middle of the sixth century B.C. in Azerbaijan. His god was Ahura-Mazdah, "the wise Lord," the official head of the Persian national pantheon. Since the days of Arixaramres, Ahura-Mazdah is sole God, but in eternal struggle with Ahriman, the Evil Spirit. From the beginning of the creation there were twin spirits of light and darkness, the good and the evil. Ahura-Mazdah is the source of truth, justice, and righteousness; Ahriman represents lies, evils, cruelty, wicked thoughts, and pride. Vile thoughts, pride and prejudice, and vicious words are the cause of mankind's destruction.

Zoroaster was never satisfied with his mission. He always asked questions, searched for the truth, and expressed his doubts:

> This I ask thee, tell me truly, Ahura,
> Who was created Father of Righteousness?
> Who fixed the path of sun of stars?
> By whom does the morn now wax, now wane?
> Who made the waters and plants?
> Who yoked swiftness to the wind and to the clouds?
> Who created good thought?
> This I ask thee, tell me truly, Ahura;
> What I proclaim, is it indeed the truth?
> Will piety aid righteousness by deeds?

---

[29] Moscati, *Ancient Middle East*, p. 293.

Will good thought announce thy kingdom?
Can he be sure of the kingdom?
Will they properly observe in word and
    deed his religion?
Who among those with whom he talks is
    righteous and who a liar?[30]

After this incursion into the world of doubts and mysticism, Zoroaster talks of his vision and believes that eventually righteousness will overcome the lie. He hopes for a confirmation of his vision from good thought. He does not believe in miracle or the redemption of sin through salvation. One's own conscience, whether of righteousness or of lie, will determine his future award and his salvation. "Righteousness separates the wise from the unwise. Those who wisely choose will proceed to the house of song, the Abode of Good Thought, the Kingdom of Good Thought, the glorious Heritage of Good Thought, built by righteousness, on which the consciences of the saviors pass to their reward."[31] Zoroaster's teachings consist of a sacred book, the Avesta, which like the Koran, the other source of the Sufi ideas, is made up of sections, differing in time and content. Only a small part of Avesta has been preserved.

The subject matter of Zoroaster's teachings can be traced through Avesta quite clearly. His thought centers on the affirmation of one God, Ahura-Mazda. "The predominance of the intellectual element in the Iranian conception of deity is confirmed by the entities which are placed alongside Ahura-Mazda: Justice, Good Thought, Good Words, Rule, Devotion, Integrity, Immortality. These are not only divinities in their own right, but also attributes or aspects of the Supreme God, who is their Creator.

"Intellectual in their personifications, Zoroaster's entities also reflect a profound moral exigency: their rule over the world means simply that rectitude and justice are the hinges of Society."[32]

Despite all the emphasis of Zoroaster on morality, he is realistic to recognize the conception of evil and wicked spirit that

---

[30] Yasna, 32–49, 51, cited by Olmstead, *History of the Persian Empire*, pp. 99–100.
[31] Ibid., 48:1–2, 9–12.
[32] Moscati, *Ancient Middle East*, pp. 295–96.

is in constant struggle with Ahura and the good forces of life.
This struggle has been with man since the beginning of the world;
but eventually good will defeat evil, and good will reign supreme.

This is Zoroaster's legacy for mankind:

> Now will I utter for whomever will listen to
>   the instruction of the initiate.
> The praise and prayers of good Thought to the
>   Lord,
> And the joy he will see, in the light, who
>   will keep them.
> Hear with your ears what is the supreme good;
> Look with clear mind on the two sides,
> Between which each man must choose for himself,
> Watchful from the beginning that the great trial
>   turn in your favor.
> In the beginning the spirits known as twins
> Are the one good and the other evil,
> In thought, in word and in deed, and between these
>   two the wise, not the foolish, can choose well,
>   when these two spirits meet.
> They established from the beginning, life and
>   not-life,
> And at the end the worse existence be for the wicked,
> And for the righteousness the better thought.
> Now when their punishment comes to the sinners,
> Then, O wise one, Thy Rule will be granted, with
>   good Thought.
> To those who delivered up evil to thy Justice, Lord!
> And may it be we who renew existence!
> O wise one, and ye other lords, O Justice, lend
>   your aid,
> That thoughts come together where understanding is
>   lacking.[33]

Zoroaster from the very beginning developed the habit of
meditation. As a young man he used to withdraw to the mountains
for days in order to meditate. "Up there among rocks and the
huge trees of primaeval forest," says Zoroaster, "good thoughts

---

[33] Yasna, 30.

came to me." He refers to good thought as Holy Spirit sent from God. The feeling that chose Zoroaster was the same as the forces that urged the Sufi poets: the pain, troubles, and tribulations of this world. In what many have conjectured to be his earliest mystical utterance, questioning the situation in which he finds himself, "the soul of the cattle" cries to God:

> For whom did you create me? And by whom did you fashion me? Upon me comes the assault of wrath and of violent power, . . . of annoyance and robbery. No other herder have I than you: teach me to find good pasture.

Like many other prophets, Zoroaster finds himself in difficulty and doubt about his mission, so appeals to Ahura-Mazda for help:

> O Mazda, aid me; obtain for me with thy good thoughts the defeat of my enemy. . . . To what land to turn? Whither shall I go? Kinsman and friend turn from me; none is found, to conciliate, to give to me; still less the false believing chiefs of the land.

> This I know, Mazda, why I am powerless: my flocks are diminished and my followers are few. Therefore, I cry to thee: Lord look upon it.[34]

Years later, Zoroaster looks back with gratitude to the periods of the meditations in which illumination first came to him:

> I will regard Thee, as holy and mighty, O wise Lord, if by thy hand, that holds the lot of false and true believers, if through thy fire's flame, the power of good Thought comes to me.

> Thee I conceived as holy, O Ahura-Mazda, when thy good Thought appeared to me and asked me: who art thou? And whose is thine allegiance?

> Then I replied: I am Zoroaster; to the false believers a sworn enemy, to the Righteous the source of might and joy.

---

[34] Yasna, 29, 44, 46, quoted by Burn, *Persia and the Greeks*.

Thee I accepted as holy, O Ahura-Mazda, when thy good
Thought appeared to me.
A difficult thing it seemed to me to spread thy faith among
people, to do that which thou didst say was best.[35]

The more Zoroaster meditates and thinks of the mystery of
this world and the destiny of man, the more his thoughts clarify:

Therefore as the First did I conceive of Thee, O Ahura-Mazda;
as the one to be adored with the mind in the creation, as the
Father of the good mind within us.

Throughout Zoroaster's works one depicts his emphasis on
meditation, wisdom, good works, righteousness, justice for all,
thrift, sacredness of the works in the fields, and universal brotherhood.

Ahura, grant people of the world, righteousness and that
Kingdom, Good Thought, whereby he may establish pleasant
dwellings and peace.
I at least have believed, Mazda, that thou canst bring this to
pass.
Where else are righteousness and good Thought and the King-
dom?
So, ye men
Welcome me for instruction, Mazda, for the great community
of the world.[36]

As the Holy One then I acknowledged Thee, Mazda-
Ahura,
When good Thought once came to me,
Best silent Thought bade me proclaim:
Let not man seek to please the many liars,
For they make all the righteous foes to thee.
Thus, Ahura, Zoroaster chooses for himself,
Mazda, whatever spirit of thine is Holiest.
May righteousness be incarnate, mighty in life's
strength,

[35] Yasna, 43, ibid.
[36] Yasna, 29, ibid.

May piety be in the kingdom that beholds the sun,
Which good Thought may be assigned Destiny to
men for their deeds.[37]

Zoroaster's religion is extremely simple. "There is no mythology; there is only the slightest trace of forms of worship and
rituals; those forms, magic and divination, which most frequently
accompany religious practice, are lacking; finally, the personnel,
the priesthood, is missing."[38]

The religion of Zoroaster and the empire of Cyrus, Darius
and Artaxerxes created in Iran a tradition and a universal outlook. It seems that the ancient Orient was able to achieve its
synthesis through the creation of a vast empire created by Cyrus
and a religion initiated by Zoroaster. Certainly, never before
had the world expressed so explicitly respect for human rights
and welfare.

"Of all the Sons of Asia," according to Jacques Duchasne-
Guillemin, "Zarathustra was the first to be adopted by the West.
His doctrine reached Greece some four centuries before Christ
was received there. It was known to Plato, to whom it must have
meant a great deal.

"Neither the Voice of Buddha, nor that of Confucious, was
to carry as far as Europe for a long time to come, and so Zoroaster
was the only one to represent the ancient Asiatic wisdom. Of the
two great currents from which the European mentality takes its
being, the Greeks and the Jewish currents, neither, can be said
to be decidedly free of all Zoroastrian contamination. . . .

"In Greece, Eudoxus of Cnidus, the contemporary and dis-
ciple of Plato, compared his master with Zoroaster. The Iranian
doctrine may be supposed to have modified or reinforced the
dualism of the Greek philosopher." Guillemin then refers to influence of Zoroastrianism on the evolution that came to light in
Judaism from the time of the Exile onward and through the mani-
fold contacts with Iran during the reign of Cyrus, Darius, and
Artaxerxes. He refers also to the new development in Palestine
of the Doctrine of Apocalypse, Kingdom of God, Last Judgment,
Resurrection, Man and Son of Man, Prince of this World, or

[37] Yasna, 43–45, ibid.
[38] Moscati, *Ancient Middle East*. p. 299.

Prince of Darkness, Righteousness, Wisdom, Justice. Zoroaster was responsible for preparing a milieu capable of receiving and interpreting the message of the life, the word and death of Jesus.[39]

Instead of a Buddha who breaks with the world, a Socrates who shocks those in office, a Jesus who renders unto Caesar the things that are Caesar's and unto God the things that are God's, one would compare Zoroaster with Confucious, traveling from one Chinese province to the other in search of the Prince who will apply his maxims of wisdom. The program that Zoroaster proposes is one of social harmony—according to the plan that God has revealed through the mouth of his prophet.

"The conception of Zoroaster's message has a truly cosmic scope."[40] He, like Sufis in later years, in his choice between communion or aloofness, pantheism or monoism, followed a midway course between the two. He understood that the essential act for every man is to choose between good and evil. The notion of morality, of good and evil, of order and chaos, did exist before him, but he discovered in them an absolute universal value. He presented us with the conception of totality of the universe. He eliminated Indo-Iranian gods, proscribed human sacrifice and the offering of the sacred liquor. In the place of all the gods he introduced a single God, the Wise Lord, Ahura Mazda. "Thus by the will of the man of genius, the traditional mythology and polytheism made way for a true theology." Its outlines are these:

> Three entities stand supreme and thus form a kind of superior triad. This is first of all the Holy Spirit. It is God, the origin of all good and example of the good choice. It is God inasmuch as he has chosen the good, life, light, and wisdom; and God inasmuch as He has created and organized the world for the good of mankind.

> The second entity, order or right, is also placed very high in the whole of the divine modalities. It is the ideal law, the divine plan, the measure of all human action, but out of all contact with man. It ranks highest in the Council of God.

---

[39] Jacques Duchesne-Guillemin, *The Hymns of Zarathustra* (London: John Murray, 1952), pp. 1, 2.

[40] Ibid., pp. 5–6.

It is quite different with the Good Mind, which is turned man, God revealing Himself to man and helping man. It is essentially active, and human virtue as much as divine virtue, for human cooperation is an essential to the divine work as divine assistance is indispensable to man.

The intimate relation which unites the Wise Lord with the first terms of the hierarchy is metaphorically expressed as parental relationship. The Wise Lord is the Father of Right, the Father of Good Mind. He is, too, the Father of the Holy Spirit with whom He is besides identical. A Father identical with his Son who is the Holy Ghost—is there not stuff for dreams, six centuries before Jesus Christ?[41]

Zoroaster constantly examines the multiple relations among different entities, such as Right, Devotion, Integrity, Good Mind, and Immortality:

> He who first by the mind filled the blessed
>     spaces with light,
> He created righteousness by his will,
> By which He upholds Best Mind.
> Thou hast, O Wise One, increased it by thy Spirit
> Which is even now one with Thee, O Lord!
> Through the mind, O Wise One, have I known Thee,
>     as the First and the Last,
> As the Father of Good Mind,
> When I perceived Thee with mine eyes as the true
>     Creator of Right,
> As the Lord in the deeds of existence.
> At the offering of veneration to thy fire,
> I will think of Righteousness, O Lord, as
>     long as I have power!
> O Wise One, Thou who, as the most Holy Spirit,
> Didst make the ox, and waters, and plants,
> Give me Immortality and Integrity,
> Strength and Endurance with the Good Mind,
>     at the Judgment.[42]

---

[41] Ibid., pp. 14–16.
[42] Yasna, 51.

Simon Peterment, a French authority on Zoroaster's teaching, asks the following pertinent question:

"Why do scholars avoid with a kind of horror representing Zoroaster as a philosopher, or as having anything, however little, to do with philosophy? Yet if there is a philosophical and universal religion, it is indeed his. Why should one not want to recognize it? Because it is very ancient? Everything is more ancient than one thinks, even, and especially, philosophy."

Zoroaster's God is intelligent, wise, righteous, and personal. He has recognized his God in a series of visions as the Holy Lord, and his holiness is different from the holiness of Jehovah. He is a friend with all compassion and wisdom and no place for vengeance or capacity for wrath and anger. "Speak to me," he says to Ahura-Mazda, "as friend to friend. Help us and grant us the support which friend would give to friend. He expects help from his God because it is part of the relationship which he conceives between God and mankind, nay of the very nature of God."[43]

"As regards western thinkers and writers," states Duchesne-Guillemin, "it is not difficult to see that Zoroaster had just what we lack most. We have knowledge, curiosity, power; but our science, our power, are inhuman. We know our wealth, but we lack the courage to choose. We feel the want of a ruler, and miss the means of re-integrating man and the universe with each other. The kind of innocence which we should most envy Zoroaster is that he conceived human values as cosmic values, that he could bring down to man's level, in the words of Paul Valery, 'The great deeds which are in heaven.' "

Thus at the close of the ancient Oriental world, the Iranians gathered cultures, religions, and civilizations together and let them flourish with tolerance, universalism, and harmony unprecedented in the history of mankind. Among the numerous achievements of the world civilization, no influence is more important to the modern world than the spirit of brotherhood and universalism and harmony originated by Cyrus and continued down through Sufi Persian literature.

---

[43] Ibid., 5–7.

Unfortunately, the Western historians have ignored that aspect of Iranian civilization and Islam which combined different peoples into a harmonious community and produced a culture, state of mind, and literature based on unity and a universal respect for human rights and values.

If proof of this be demanded, one has but to reflect that it is Persian liberalism that allows the reconstitution of the Hebrew religious community in Palestine, with all the consequences that follow from it. In the religious field, Zarathustra's teaching achieves the highest point of ancient oriental intellectualism. In his conception of the universe, the forces of logic are already active.[44]

---

The ideas of Manes and the Manichaeans have also left their impacts on the Sufi literature.

Manes, the founder of the Manichaean religion was born in A.D. 215. His mission was a protest against the Zoroastrian Church, which by then had become oppressive and corrupt. In his system, Manes was eclectic; but he borrowed materials and ideas from ancient Babylonian, Buddhist, and Christian religions. But his main endeavor, according to Gibon, was to reconcile Zoroastrianism with other creeds in general and Christianity in particular. This attempt brought him persecution and hatred from both Christians and Zoroastrians. They "pursued him with equal and unrelenting hatred."

Information concerning the life, doctrines and writings of Manes are both Eastern and Western, but the former is more available and reliable than that contained in the writings of St. Augustine and other Western historians, which are both biased and distorted.[45]

According to Al-Yagubi, Manes introduced dualism and opposed many aspects of the works of the Zoroastrian Church. He

44 Moscati, *Ancient Middle East*, pp. 305–6.
45 Reliable Sources: Fihrist (composed by Al Biruni, A.D. 987), Al-Yagubi, and Tabari.

contended that "the Controller of the Universe was twofold, and that there were two eternal principles, Light and Darkness; two creators, the Creator of Good and the Creator of Evil. The Darkness and the Light, each one of them, connotes in itself five ideas: color, taste, smell, touch, and sound, whereby these two do hear, see and know; and what is good and beneficial is from the Light, while what is hurtful and calamitous is from Darkness."

Manes's written works, according to Yagubi, were collected in several books: *The Treasure of Living, Shapurgan, The Book of Guidance and Planning, Book of Secrets, Book of Giants,* and the Twelve Gospels, each named after one of the letters of the alphabet. The latter dealt with prayers and deliverance of the soul.

The account of Manes's life given in the Fihrist is much fuller and dramatic. According to the Fihrist's account, before Manes's birth the angel Tawm appeared to his mother and gave her the tiding of her son's mission. He traveled in India and China and he was barbarously executed in A.D. 276.

Although Manes's doctrines had their roots in the religion of Zoroaster, they vehemently opposed the Zoroastrian Church, which at Manes's time was national, militant, materialistic, and imperialistic. "Manes's teachings were cosmopolitan, quietist, spiritual, universal, ascetic, and unworldly. The two systems stood in essential antagonism and, for all their external resemblance, were inevitably hostile and radically opposed."[46]

> In general the Zoroastrian religion, for all its elaborately systematized spiritual hierarchies, presents itself as an essentially material religion, in the sense that it encouraged its followers to be faithful and multiply and replenish the earth, and to sow the seed and reap the harvest with enduring toil.[47]

The Manichaeans, on the other hand, believed that the combination of Light and Darkness that gave rise to the material universe was essentially evil, and strengthened the power of corruption in this world. "It was only good insofar as it afforded a

---

[46] E. G. Browne, *A Literary History of Persia,* vol. 1 (London: T. Fisher Unwin, 1909), pp. 156–62.
[47] Darmesteter's English translation of Avesta, vol. 1, p. 46.

means of escape and return to its proper sphere to that portion
of the Light which had become entangled in the Darkness; and
when this deliverance was, so far as possible, effected, the angels
who supported the heavens and upheld the earth would relax
their hold, and the whole material universe would collapse, and
the final conflagration would mark the redemption of the Light
and its final disassociation from the irredeemable and indestruc-
tible Darkness."[48]

The Manichaeans recognized not only Zoroaster and Buddha
as divine messengers, but also Christ, though here they distinguished between the true Christ, who was, in their view, an Ap-
parition from the world of Light, and the Christ created by the
Church as the Son of Mary who was crucified. It is interesting
that this belief of the Manichaean was adopted by the Prophet
Mohammed in the Koran:

> And for their saying, "Verily we slew the Messiah, Jesus, the
> Son of Mary, the Apostle of God; but they did not slay him or
> crucify him, but the matter was made doubtful to them (or
> similitude was made for them). And verily those who differ
> about Him are in doubt concerning Him; they have no knowl-
> edge concerning Him, but only follow an opinion. They did
> not kill Him, for sure; but God raised Him up unto Himself;
> for God is mighty and wise."[49]

Manes showed a universal and tolerant attitude toward the
peoples of different faith. He never considered his doctrines the
only true faith and expressed great respects for other religions
and ideas:

> Wisdom and deeds have always from time to time been brought
> to mankind by the messengers of God. So in one age they have
> been brought by the messenger of God called Buddha to India,
> in another by Zoroaster to Persia, in another by Jesus to the
> West. Thereafter this revelation has come down, this prophecy
> in this last age, through me, Mani, the messenger of the God
> of Truth to Babylonia.[50]

[48] Browne, *Literary History of Persia*, p. 161.
[49] Koran, Sura, Mary 4, 5:156.
[50] Al Biruni, Fihrist, translated by Browne, *Literary History of Persia*, vol. 1, p. 163.

The Manichaeans were divided into five groups: the Muallimun, or teachers, referred to as "The Sons of Tenderness"; the Mushammasun, or those illuminated by the rays of the Sun, called "The Sons of Knowledge"; The Qissisiun, or priests, called "The Sons of Understanding"; The Siddigiun, or faithful, called "The Sons of the Unseen"; and the Sammaun, or hearers, called "The Sons of Intelligence." The Manichaeans were ordered to pray and to avoid idol worship, falsehood, covetousness, hatred, prejudice, murder, theft, fornication, and teaching of all materials that cause deception, anger, discord, hypocrisy in religion, magic, and negligence in responsibility and daily life.

Manes's doctrines differed in principle with the ideas of the prevalent churches of his time by assigning primacy to human mind and heart, and by accepting universalism and brotherhood of all faiths. He faced strong opposition from institutions and churches that emphasized the supremacy and monopoly of their own faith.

To the principle of a spiritual world, Manes added belief in the three Supreme Essences: God, the King of Paradise of Lights, His Light, His Power, and His Wisdom; fasting for seven days in each month; and the acceptance of "the three seals," called by St. Augustine[51] *"the Signacula Oris, Manum et Sinus,"* that is the renunciation of "evil words, evil deeds, and evil thoughts, and corresponding to the *Hukht, Huvarsat* and *Humat* [good words, good deeds, and good thoughts] of the Zoroastrian religion."[52]

Although Manes and his followers faced fierce persecution both in the East and the West at the hands of Zoroastrians and Christians (from the beginning until the extermination of the unfortunate Albigenses in the thirteenth century), their ideas and doctrines continued to exercise an immense influence on religion, literature, and Sufi ideas throughout the world.

---

[51] St. Augustine was a follower of Manes before he accepted Christianity.
[52] Browne, *Literary History of Persia,* p. 165.

The other source of Sufi universalism could be traced to Islam. "Islam is a harmony of idealism and positivism. It is also a unity of the eternal verities of freedom, equality and solidarity. It has no fatherland; and there can be no Turkish, Arab, Persian, or Indian Islam."[53] Muhammad in his mission encourages the concepts of the unity of human origin and a sense of the reality of time and life as a continuous movement in time:

> Oh mankind; Be careful of your duty to your Lord who created you from a single person, and of him created his mate and from these twain hath spread abroad a multitude of men and women.[54]

Muhammad also connected his mission with the teachings of the prophets of Israel and Christ. He states that at first mankind lived a natural life. There was neither mutual rivalry nor enmity among them. They were content with their natural collective life. It was at a subsequent stage when they multiplied, that economic pressure gave rise to conflict of interests, resulting in the oppression of the weak. As a result society was divided into groups and classes, each fighting and hating the other. The situation demanded a message of truth and justice. It was thus that the door of Revelation opened. First came Abraham, followed by Moses, Christ, and Muhammad. They were all Rasul, messengers of God, and their message to mankind was the divine message of truth:

> Mankind was but one people; and God sent prophets to announce glad tidings and to warn; and He sent down with them the Book of Truth, that it might decide the dispute of men.[55]

The message of all the prophets, according to the Koran, was one and the same and was not meant for any particular race, climate, country, or people. It had a universal application for mankind. No corner of the world has remained outside this message:

[53] Aziz Ahmad, *Studies in Islamic Culture* (Oxford: Clarence Press, 1964), p. 69.
[54] Koran 4:1.
[55] Koran 2:213.

Nor had there been a people unvisited by a messenger. Assuredly, thou [Muhammad] art a warnee. And every people hath had its guide.

And to every people have we sent an apostle saying: Serve God and turn away from forces of mischief and disorder.

And truly this religion is one religion; I am your Lord.

To you [Muhammad] that prescribed the faith which God commended unto Noah, and which we have revealed to thee, and which we commended unto Abraham and Moses and Jesus, saying,

Observe this faith, and be not divided into sects.[56]

The Koranic argument is: God has given you all but one form—the human form, and welded you into one community. But you have divided yourselves into so-called races and have kept yourselves aloof from one another, and have carved out accordingly different homelands. You have divided yourselves into countless nations, each feuding and fighting for its own selfish interests. Dispersed as we are under different colors, this has presented us with another excuse for mutual hatred. We have also developed and created classes of the rich and the poor, the master and the servant, the touchables and the untouchables, the strong and the weak, the high and the low, the lord and serf, labor and management.

In such a situation, is there anything that can bring us all together? The Koran answers that there is: respect and tolerance for individuals and their faiths. Despite all internal and external differences, we are all the children of the same God who created us in his own image. He made the entire globe our home, and his will is that we serve our fellow men with compassion, care, and consideration:

For everyone a side to turn to. Better, therefore,
    vie one with another in good works.

---

56 Koran 2:148.

God will gather you all together, for
God hath power over all things.

Righteousness is not that you turn your faces [in prayer]
towards the east or the west; but righteousness is this that we
believeth in God . . . and for the love of God giveth of his
wealth to his kindred and to the orphans, and to the needy
and to the way-farer, and to those who asked and to effect
the freedom of the slave, and observeth prayer and being
faithful to their engagements when they have engaged in
them, and endureth with fortitude, poverty, distress and moments of peril—these are those who are true in their faith
and these are they who are truly righteous.[57]

When Muhammad started to preach his mission, the world
was divided between the Persian empire and the two Roman empires. In Persia, already there had been revolts by Mani and
Mazdek against the corruption of the court and leaders of the
Zoroastrian religion. The Christian world also was chaotic and
divided by two centers, one in Rome and the other in Constanti-
nople. The heads of the two churches spent more time in excom-
municating each other than in spreading Christ's message of love.
Every religious group denied salvation to every other merely on
the basis of outward rituals. They fought each other, destroyed
life and property in the name of God. Muhammad, with his
vision of universalism, warned against this practice. He stated
that ritual was not religion, and nobody had a right to claim
that he alone represented the truth. God needs no public relations
agent. True religion was love, service, and tolerance.

Then Muhammad asks,

Why do you give so much importance to ceremonial? God
had prescribed different ceremonies at different times and
for different countries. Whatever was appropriate to a particular situation was prescribed. Had God so desired, He would
have made all mankind of but one pattern. But that evidently
was not His purpose. Variations were called for, and it did
take place. But this variation should not form the ground for
conflict between one person and another. What really mattered

---

[57] Koran 2:177.

in this context was righteous action to which every varying ceremonial was subsidiary.[58]

"To each among you have we prescribed a law". This is the fundamental principle of Islam, tolerance and understanding for other creeds and ideologies:

Revile not those whom they call on beside God lest they in their ignorance despitefully revile him. We have so fashioned the nature of man that they like the deeds they do. After all, they shall return to their Lord, and he will declare to them what their actions have been.[59]

Verily, those who believe in Islam and they who follow the Jewish religion, and the Christians, and the Sabaons—whosoever believeth in God and the last day, and doeth that which is right, shall have their reward with their Lord: fear shall not come upon them, neither shall they give.[60]

The prophet Muhammad, in his observation of the troubled and tormented world, realized that no lasting stability and concord of nations would be possible without a concert of the religions. His idea of world religious synthesis, at the time, was attacked by different religious groups, including his own people.

As generally happens in history, an established religion clashes with the new upstart faith. Muhammad and his faith at the beginning were the objects of attack from pagans, Christians, Zoroastrians, and Jewish establishments. He was even threatened with death and had to leave Mecca for Medina. His sufferings and hardships at Mecca, his travel experiences, his visits to the Christian monasteries, and his discussions with Jewish teachers convinced Muhammad that there can be no world civilization without some kind of harmony among different religions customs and cultures throughout the world. So Muhammad, in his luminous mind, examines all the dominant religions of his time and asks them, "Why are you fighting each other, if you are seeking the same God and the same truth?" Religion, according to Mu-

---

[58] Koran 5:51.
[59] Koran 6:108.
[60] Koran 2:59.

hammad, is man's concern for ultimate value and meaning in
life. The world cannot survive without belief in God and harmonious cooperation pointing toward ultimate unity and service.
No nobler view of universal humanity is possible to conceive of
than the one advanced in the following verses:

> Moreover the Jews say, "The Christians lean on nought" "on
> nought lean the Jews", say the Christians, yet both read the
> scripture. So with like words say they have no knowledge of
> the scripture. But on the day of requital, God shall judge be-
> tween them as to that in which they differ.[61]

Unity of man is the primary purpose of religion. The message of God delivered by his prophets is universal, and states that
mankind was in reality one people and one community, and that
there was but one God for all of them, and they should worship
him together and live as members of one family. Such was the
message that every religion delivered:

> We sent Noah to his people. He said, O my people, serve God!
> You have no God but Him.

> Then we raised after them another generation.
> And we sent to them an apostle from among themselves, say-
> ing, "Serve God! Ye have
>     no other God but Him."
> Then we sent Moses and his brother Aaron.
> And we made the Son of Mary and his mother as our repre-
> sentative.[62]

> Verily we have revealed to thee as we revealed to Noah and the
> prophets after him, and as we revealed to Abraham and Ismail
> and Isaac, and Jacob, and the tribes, and Jesus, and Job and
> Jonah, Aaron and Solomon; and to David we gave psalms.

> Of some apostles we have told thee before: of other apostles
> we have not told thee.
> O ye apostles! Truly this your religion is the one religion.
> And I am your Lord.[63]

---

[61] Koran 2:113.
[62] Koran 23:23; 32; 45; 50.
[63] Koran 42:13; 4:163; 4:161-2; 23:51.

Then the Koran, addressing Muhammad, in the name of God states: "These are those whom God has guided. So, follow therefore what had guided them."

According to the above statement, the first principle of Islam is to recognize the founders of all religions and endorse their teaching, which basically is all the same:

> We believe in God, and in what hath been sent down to us, and what hath been sent down to Abraham, and Ismail, and Isaac, and Jacob, and the tribes and what was given to Moses, and Jesus, and the prophets from their Lord. We make no difference between them. And to the Lord we are resigned.[64]

The expression "we make no difference between them" appears several times in different chapters of the Koran. Its purpose is to discourage the idea of the chosen people or chosen religions. It refutes the theory of religious supremacy. It disapproves of the tendency of regarding one prophet greater than another or accepting one and rejecting other prophets.

The Koran calls upon everyone who cares to follow the way laid down by God to accept without discrimination all the prophets and all the scriptures revealed to them and the basic truth which they all contain, and to accept it wherever found in whatever language it is expressed."[65]

> The apostle believeth in that which hath been sent down from his Lord, as do the faithful also. They all believe in God and his angels and his books and his apostles: We make no distinction between any of His apostles.[66]

The divine truth, contends the Koran, is a universal gift from God. It is not the monopoly of any race or any religion or language. God can hear you whether you speak in Latin, Greek, Persian, English, or Arabic. The myths about prayer or rituals in an exclusive language are invented by those who try to use religion and God for their selfish interests. Divine truth is indi-

---

[64] Koran 3:78.
[65] See Abdul Kalam Azad, *The Tar Juman Al-Quoran*, vol. 2 (New Delhi: Asia Publishing House, 1962), pp. 150–72.
[66] Koran 2:285.

visible. Only rascals and scoundrels advocate religious or racial hatreds. Truth bears no religious or national stamps. Like the midday sun, it shines in every corner of the world, and shines equally on every individual.

The truth of God is but one and is meant for all and was indeed given to everyone. But in implementing it, mankind had divided itself into numerous groups. The time has come, states the Koran, when we should all return to universal mission of man and put an end to tribalism and religious, racial, and class conflicts. The universal mission is achieved only through devotion to God, service to his people, and righteous living:

> Every group thinks that salvation in the hereafter is exclusively reserved for them, and that unless one gets into their fold, one cannot obtain salvation. O prophet! Such are their ignorant expectations. . . .

> There is no doubt that the path of salvation is always open to all. That path is one of faith and action and not of groupism.[67]

Tribalism and group fanaticism were very dominant in Arabia, at the time of the Prophet Muhammad. Each group maintained its own place of worship and denied admission to others. Every sect tried to destroy the house of worship of his rivals. Muhammad warned against this practice:

> And think over! Who committeth a greater wrong than he who hinders God's name from being taken in His places of prayer and attempts to ruin them? It is not for such as these to enter therein save in fear of God. . . .

> And note! Whether it is the East or the West, it is all God's.

> The worship of Him is not conditioned
> By any place or direction.
> Whichever side you turn to God, turns He to you. Without doubt God is omnipresent and omniscient.[68]

---

[67] Koran, chapter on Cow, v. 111–12.
[68] Koran, chapter on Cow, v. 114, 115.

Muhammad emphasizes the universality of man by addressing him as the "Son of Adam"; on the day of Judgment God will address a particular individual: "O Son of Adam."

The quality that distinguishes man from the mere animal is his universal feelings, compassion and care, which are a reflection of the attributes of God. Perfection is to be reached by expressing in one's life more and more of these divine qualities.

Referring to this aspect of universality of man, the Koran states:

> Then God shaped man and breathed of His spirit into him, and gave you all hearing and seeing and hearts.

This verse explains clearly that man, regardless of his color, or creed, is created equal, and his position in the scale of life is so exalted that God himself has breathed his breath into him. In other words, man has been created with the attributes of God, and, therefore, he should practice these attributes:

> Who master their anger and forgive others!
> God loveth the doers of good.[69]

It is a matter of profound regret that the people (including Muslims) have failed to appreciate Muhammad's acceptance of other religions and disregarded his often repeated principle of the universalism of man. In this inability of Muslims, Christians, Jews, and followers of other religions to appreciate the universalism of the messages of their Bibles lies the tragedy of man. Clearly churches have done a great wrong in fueling the fire of the religious feuds, and the unsympathetic critics have made no attempt to show the harmonious aspects of all the religions of the world. Muhammad, being cognizant of this tragedy, attempted to point out that the downfall of man is due to the fact that he has tried to make distinctions between religions. This attitude is summed up in the following statement:

> We make no difference between the prophets of God, and we are Muslims resigned to God.[70]

---

[69] Koran 3:128.
[70] Koran 3:78.

The Koran's description of Jesus, his birth, his life, and his teaching, is laudatory:

> And we will make him [Christ] a sign to mankind, and a mercy from us.
> And we gave him [Christ] the Evangel, and we filled the hearts of those who followed him with kindness and compassion.[71]

> And we gave him [Christ] the Evangel with its guidance and light, confirmatory of the preceding law [Torah], a guidance and warning of those who fear God.[72]

The Koran also warns against confusing the principle of religion with the actions of those who call themselves the trustees and masters of temples, churches, synagogues, or mosques. The aim of all the religions has been to inculcate in man the sense of dislike for evil, but the establishments have tried to create hatred among men. Prophets instructed us to live a decent life of love and service. They certainly did not ask anyone to hate and oppress people whose faith and belief are different from their own. The message of all the religions is that we should love our fellow men and avoid evils and action that hurt others. Since there is so little difference between the teaching of the Bible and the Koran, and their injunctions are the same, why should the followers of these books fight continuously?

According to Muhammad all these messages are universal. Only the style employed in the expression and the occasion for the utterance varies. Christ stressed the need for love and purification of the heart. He did not attempt to lay down any law, for the law of Moses was there, and he did not choose to alter it. The Koran, however, presents ethics and law simultaneously. It combines love and compassion of Christ with the law and order of Moses.

In the first place, it calls upon man to develop a talent for compassion and forgiveness, because it regards them as the basis on which all piety and righteousness should rest. Secondly, it

---

[71] Koran 19:21.
[72] Koran 5:50.

keeps open the door for retaliation in unavoidable contingencies. Thirdly, it is careful to make it clear that "there is more pleasure in forgiveness than in retaliation." This attitude is the fundamental creed for all the religions.

Muhammad was grieved that man throughout the ages worshipped no religion but himself. He used the words *truth, God,* and *religion* for his own selfish interest; he has always adopted the same style and raised the same slogans to serve him:

> And those who have no knowledge of the sacred scriptures, as for example the polytheists of Arabia say: "If this teaching is from God, why is it that God speaketh not direct to us or why is it that He doth not send some wonderful token to us." Mark! What these people say is exactly what had already been said by those who had gone before them. Like minds are they. Anyway, if these people are really after token, they will have, in the first instance, to develop the talent to recognize tokens.[73]

To Muhammad this token of universalism was the teaching of the prophets, beginning with Abraham and ending with him. He argues that the various groups into which men have resolved themselves are all the creation of human perversity. Group formation engenders the spirit of exclusivism among its members and discourages harmony and search for reality. Few people pay regard to what one believes or how one lives. Attention is paid only to one thing—the group and its interests. Muhammad tried to fight the spirit of my religion and yours, my group and yours. He connected man's religion and universality to Abraham, who was respected by the Jews, Christians, and Arabs. The way of Abraham, stated Muhammad, was not the groupism or feud between the so-called Christians, Muslims, and the Jews:

> This is the way of Abraham. Is there any one that turneth away from the way of Abraham except one who deliberately chooses to fool himself? Assuredly, we have chosen him for distinction in this world and indeed he will be among the righteous in the world to come.[74]

[73] Azad, *Tar Juman Al-Quoran,* vol. 2, pp. 80–82.
[74] Koran, chapter on Cow, v. 130.

The Koran points out that Prophet Muhammad's message of universality of man was as important and profound as his message on the unity of God:

> I have come to acknowledge the universal truth given to all prophets. Should you be a Jew and believe in the Torah, then, I am here to say that your Book is truly from God. I have come to endorse it and revive the truth it contains. Should you be a Christian, do I deny the Evangel? I have come to make you act truly on the Evangel. If you are a follower of Abraham, then bear in mind that my mission is wholly his own. If you are a follower of another prophet or of the founder of another religion then it is not my wish to turn you away from him. I should like you to be more staunchly devoted to him.[75]

> O, prophet! Say to these people:
> Our way is nothing but one of devotion to God.
> Do you quarrel with us concerning God?
> Or do you disapprove of all devotion to God, especially when you are aware that He is our Lord, even as He is your Lord?
> To us then the result of our deeds, and to you the result of your deeds. For our part, we are but His devoted servants.[76]

The idea of proselytizing, borrowed later from the Christian Church, had little appeal to the Prophet Muhammad:

> There is no compulsion in religion. That is not the way to create faith which is but an inward force. Without doubt the right way is clearly distinguishable from the wrong way. [It is for everyone to choose one of them.][77]

The apostles! At the level of prophethood, all are of equal rank; but from the standpoint of special roles attached to them severally, God has bestowed on some more distinction than on some others. Of these, a few there were with whom He held converse by delivering them to His book. There are others in accordance with the times and circumstances in which they had been called upon to function as prophets. To Jesus, Son of

---

[75] Azad, *Tar Juman Al-Quoran*, vol. 2, p. 52.
[76] Koran, The Albagarah, v. 139.
[77] Koran, The Albagarah, v. 139.

Mary, we granted clear signs and conveyed our aid to him through the holy spirit of revelation. . . .
It was so decreed that mankind should not be pressed into but a single pattern and that every one should be left free to pursue the path one cared to choose for himself. So it so happened that mankind fell into disputes; some followed the path of belief and some of unbelief. Had God willed differently He would have denied to them the power of disagreement. But God doth what he willeth; no one can comprehend His purposes.[78]

On many occasions in the Koran, Prophet Muhammad appeals to different sects to forget about their differences and to agree on principles acceptable to all parties:

O prophet! Say to the Jews and the Christians: O people of the Book! Let us not wrangle over what may be regarded as controversial subject. Let us at least agree on that which is recognised alike by you and by us, i.e., that we worship none but God and associate nothing with Him, and take not each other as lord to the exclusion of God.

Remember, Abraham was neither a Jew nor a Christian nor a follower of any sectarian creed. On the other hand, he was one staunch in faith, resigned to God, and one who would not let anything affect the singleness of his devotion to God.

Of men who should claim the closest relation to Abraham are those who followed him in his time as well as this prophet, and those who believe in him, and not those, who have split up his faith into Judaism and Christianity and denied in practice the unity of God. And remember that God is the protector of the faithful.[79]

The Koran, on several occasions draws attention to a fundamental doctrine of Islam that all prophets sponsored but one universal way of life. That is why every succeeding prophet had to affirm that he was merely confirming what had been done by his predecessors. When the way of God is universal and when

---

[78] Azad, *Tar Juman Al-Quoran*, vol. 2, pp. 119–20.
[79] Koran, Al Imran, v. 64–65, 67–68.

prophets represent a universal message, to differentiate one religion from the other or to accept one opposite another is to deny the entire line of prophets or the universal character of man. According to the Koran, the way of God or religion is nothing but conformity to the laws of life at work in nature. All that there is on the earth or in the heavens scrupulously obeys these laws of nature. This divine law of nature is universal. Why do you object to this universal law of nature? This law offers universal guidance to mankind. Do not destroy it by constituting yourself into groups and sects and fighting those who do not follow you. Follow the divine law of universality, as members of one family, caring for those who need your care and assisting those who are in need of assistance. "No distinction we make between any religion and to God we are resigned."

No way of life, sought after by one, other than the way of acknowledging all prophets who have sponsored the way of truth, shall be acceptable and he who follows any other way shall in the next world be among the lost.[80]

The things that matter in life, according to Prophet Muhammad, are the principles and the values of life that it upholds, and not the personalities who expound it, however highly placed. A personality is of importance only as one who expounds a universal principle, contributing to the welfare of all mankind. It is because of the ideas that people express that we follow or reject them. Truth is not truth because somebody expounds it. It is so on its own merits.

Muhammad is no more than an apostle.
Apostles before him have passed away.

O ye who believe!
Exercise patience, and vie in patience and stand united and be mindful of God that it may be well with you.[81]

One of the greatest tragedies in history has been religious fanaticism, resulting in wars, destruction, and holocaust. More

---

[80] Koran, Al-Imran, v. 85.
[81] Koran, Al-Imran, v. 144, 200.

crimes have been committed in the name of religion than in the name of any other issue in history. Muhammad, witnessing religious feuds of his time, experiencing all kinds of oppression and humiliation himself, warned the world:

O people of the Book [Jews, Christians, and Muslims] do not be intemperate in the matter of religion, and of God speak nothing but truth. Believe therefore in God and his apostles. . . .

O Muslims! For the sake of God, stand up to uphold justice and let not ill-will toward any people impel you to deviate from justice. Act justly. This indeed is akin to piety.[82]

Muhammad, warning against religious fanatacism, stated that the aim of Jews, Christians, and Muslims alike is no doubt the same: man's perfection or salvation. The very language that they all use in teaching us to reach this aim is often identical. Even when their language indicates variations, the different courses of thought that are uppermost in each discipline, the universal aim and the final end, are still the same. That aim and end is "that we might be partakers of divine nature." It is rather interesting that at the beginning of the Prophet Muhammad's mission, Christians, Jews, and pagans ridiculed him and claimed superiority for their respective faiths. Muhammad protested, explaining their opposition was based on injustice and misrepresentation. He emphasizes time and again that the aim and end of all the religions is one and the same, and this aim and end is august and admirable.

Still he suggested that they pursue the aims by different courses. There is what is called *Din* and there is what is called *Sharia,* and there is also what is called *Minhaj. Din,* or religion, the aim of all prophets, is universal and the same. It is the way of life and devotion to God and of righteous living. *Sharia,* or the Law, and *Minhaj,* or the ritual, form the program or details of this way of living and devotion, prescribed to implement the principles implicit in *Din. Din* is universal and one, and it is this which has been enjoined on every man by every revealed faith.

---

[82] Koran, Almaida, v. 8.

But the law and rituals have assumed different forms, for the reason of the climate, education, environments, and the way people react to situations in different countries.

Unfortunately, in the course of this development, man lost sight of the reality of universal faith and concentrated his attention on law and rituals, and this inevitably led to the division of mankind into diverse groups, each denying the universal truth to every other person. The Koran says:

O you people of the world:
surely, we have created you of a male and a female, and made you into tribes and families that you may know each other; surely the most honorable of you with God is the one among you who is most virtuous. Surely, Allah is knowing and aware.[83]

The above verse is the best expression of Prophet Muhammad's idea of the universality of man. It is not addressed to Arabs or Muslims, but to all the people of the world as members of a family equal in the eyes of their Creator. Their divisions into nations, tribes, and families should not result in religious, racial, national, or social prejudice. Superiority in this universal world, according to the Koran, does not depend on family, wealth, rank, title, creed, or color, but on virtue, love, and moral integrity. Virtue and love must always be put before glory and ambition. Glory in this world is the shadow of virtue. Therefore, virtue and love must be the cornerstone of the edifice of our society. Whoever abandons virtue and love ends up with a bare and miserable life that only resembles that of the brute beasts that follow headlong their appetite, which to them is their only law.[84]

The uppermost idea with Prophet Muhammad is submission and obedience to the will of one universal God. It changes nothing in Judaism or Christianity. Self-conquest, self-devotion, following the will of a universal God as Creator of all people are the fundamental ideas of the discipline that Prophet Muhammad called *Din* (religion). Islam claims that it combined Judaic devotion to

---

83 Koran 49:13.
84 Nasrollah S. Fatemi, Faramarz S. Fatemi, and Fariborz S. Fatemi, *Sufism: Message of Brotherhood, Harmony, and Hope* (South Brunswick and New York: A. S. Barnes and Co., Inc., 1976).

one God and his laws with Christian love and compassion, adding the idea of universality and equality of man, whose mission is patient continuance in well-doing and self-conquest.

This should not come to us as a surprise, since Judaism, Christianity, and Islam are profound and admirable manifestations of man's life, tendencies, and powers, and all of them aim at a like final result. Any divergence is not the fault of the founders, but the result of selfish interests of the groups, sects, and denominations. These public relations men of God have engendered much feud and conflict that, in the words of the Prophet Zechariah, "has raised up thy sons, O Zion, against thy sons, O Greece." These differences, whether they were the result of fanaticism, ignorance, or selfishness and greed, have left their tragic legacy and their disastrous mark on all the history of mankind and its development.

Judaism, Christianity, Islam, and other faiths arose out of the needs of humanity and addressed their mission to satisfying those needs. This connection and the universal thinking of the ancient faiths and ideas are so profound that both Cyrus, a Zoroastrian, and Muhammad, a Muslim, are "terribly at ease in Zion." It is unfortunate that the Jewish, Christian, Muslim, and even Zoroastrian churches have always been severely preoccupied with an awful sense of impossibility of being at ease in each other's religion.

> In the beginning, mankind were not divided into groups. On the other hand, they were but one community, and then it so happened that they divided themselves into separate groups. So God raised prophets among them to give them glad tidings of the good results that flow from good deeds and to warn them of the evil consequences which flow from evil deeds. With these prophets was also sent down the Book of Truth that they might, under its guidance, resolve their differences and unite together to pursue but one common way of righteous living. But they fell at variance, not because the clear instructions of God had not reached them, but because they were envious of each other, despite their awareness of the revelations having reached them.[85]

---

[85] Koran, chapter on Cow, v. 213.

At the time of the Prophet Muhammad there was a belief among different religious groups that whatever had been enjoined on them in regard to the observance of honesty should be observed only in relation to the people of their own tribe or faith, and that it was not necessary to observe them in relation to others. They regarded it lawful to defraud others in every way. The Prophet Muhammad protested against this tradition and expressed that dishonesty in any form and against any group is, after all, dishonesty. The difference in religion does not alter the nature of good and evil, honesty and dishonesty:

> Among the people of the Book are some, every one of whom will restore even a large treasure to thee shouldst thou entrust it to him; and among them also there are some, none of whom will restore to thee even a dinar, shouldst thou entrust it to him, unless thou are pressing in thy demand on him. This is because they say: "We owe no responsibility to keep faith with the pagans", and thus they foist a lie on God and they do it knowingly.
> Every one is responsible for what he does, be it good or evil. That is the Law of God.[86]

The Koran, in this case and on many other occasions, draws attention to a fundamental doctrine of Islam that all the prophets sponsored but one way of life. That is why every church should accept what had been announced by other prophets, because the way of God is but one and the different prophets have together formed but one chain of command. To differentiate one from the other, or to accept one and reject another, is to deny the entire command of God.

Even in this last quarter of the twentieth century ecumenical councils exclude Muslims, Jews, Buddhists, and Hindus, ignoring the fact that these groups constitute sixty-five percent of the total population of the world. In the United States we talk about religious unity and harmony, while the so-called National Conference excludes Orthodox Christians, the Muslims, the Buddhists, and the Hindus. How can there be a national conference of religions if sixty-five percent of the population of the world is

---

[86] Koran, Al-Imran, v. 75–76.

excluded? If we accept that the best man in the eyes of God is he who most tries to perfect himself, why should the traditions of Christian, Muslim, or Jew prevent a man to sit at the same council table with his fellow man? Why should religion or nationality take priority over humanity, which is the most fundamental principle of creation? God created man as a human being in his image and as a member of one family. Traditions and words such as *religion* and *nationality* are man made, and they are the antithesis of the doctrine of universality of man, and the oneness of God.

It was because of this conflict that the Sufis revolted against all the churches and created a synthesis borrowed from Judaism, Christianity, Zoroastrianism, Buddhism, Hellenism, and Islam. They made very clear that Sufism was not a new religion, but a way of life to get rid of religious prejudice, ignorance, and hatred, to see things as they are, and by seeing them as they are, to see them in their beauty and in the simple and attractive ideal that humanity presents to us. Sufism attempts to acquaint us with the simplicity and charm of this universal world. Sufis believe that human life is invested with a kind of aerial ease, clearness, and decency. It is full of what we call sweetness and light. Sufis try to minimize religious, racial, and national conflicts and to occupy our minds with beauty, beneficence, and blessings of this world. "The happiest man," according to Sadi, "is he who desires little and enjoys life by perfecting his mind." This life has so many simple, spontaneous, and unsophisticated moments that it will fill us with joy and hope when we pay attention and take advantage of them. Sufis argue that all the churches have built walls and created obstacles to human universality and perfection through their emphasis on sin, salvation, and superiority of their faith.

In the words of Rumi:

> The faithful are many, but their faith is one;
> Their bodies are numerous, but their soul is one.
> Besides the understanding and soul which is in
>     the ox and the ass,
> Man has another intelligence and soul.

Again, in man as the owner of the Divine breath,
There is a soul other than the human soul.
The animal soul does not possess oneness;
Do not seek oneness from that spirit.
If its owner eats bread, his neighbor is not
    filled; if he bear a load, his neighbor
    does not become laden;
Nay, but he rejoices at his neighbor's death
    and dies of envy when he sees his neighbor
    prosperous.
The souls of wolves and dogs are separate; the
    souls of the lions of God [men of faith]
    are united.
When you remove the walls, all these scattered
    lights are one and the same.
When the bodily houses have no foundation
    remaining, the faithful remain one soul.[87]

The Sufis never advocated the unification of the living religions of the world, although they are all "already fused together
to speak, at the top," through their showing of certain universal
truths. Each must retain its integral identity and emphasize what
it presents best, and the result will be a unity in diversity. To
every man, the West and the East alike will naturally contribute
whatever is universal in their culture, no longer as Western or
Eastern, but as a member of a universal family. The plurality of
religions, to Rumi, is nothing but a kind of optical illusion.

It took many years of research and traveling for Arnold Toynbee to discover Sufism, its roots and its universal appeals. In the
earlier volumes of his study, Toynbee believes that civilization
was to be saved by Christianity alone. This idea labeled him as
the exponent of religious imperialism. On the same Christocentric
principle, he also rated Shiite Muslims over the more orthodox
Sunnite. Here he showed his ignorance of the true meaning of
Islam. His knowledge of Sunnite Islam was based on perversities
he witnessed in the history of the Ottoman Empire. He omitted
Judaism until years later, when his tallies of the higher religions
included Judaism, Zoroastrianism, and Himalayan Buddhism in
his select company.

[87] Rumi, translated by R. A. Nicholson, quoted in Fatemi et al., *Sufism*, p. 110.

Centuries before Toynbee's research and his new education, Sufis declared that the ways unto God are as numerous as the number of people living in this world:

> In cell and cloister, monastery and synagogue,
> one lies
> In dread of Hell, one dreams of Paradise.
> But none that know the secrets of the Lord
> Have sown their hearts with such like fantasies.

Hafiz, the Sufi poet of the fourteenth century, ridicules those who are seeking salvation in the labels of Judaism, Christianity, Islam, or Buddhism:

> What care if sober or drunk, every man is
> seeking the friend;
> What care if in mosque or church, each place
> is the house of love,
> What care if in Hell or Heaven we alight,
> if the friend be there?
> What care if in mosque or church we kneel,
> if our prayer be true?

Shabastari, the author of *Gulshan Raz*, believes that the goal of man should be altogetherness in which we walk together creatively and to which we all contribute, a universal idea established not through fusion of religions, but through fellowship.

In their promotion of the idea of universality of man, Sufis advocated a rebellion against the authoritarian, dogmatic, inhumane streak in the so-called monotheistic religions, rather than against religious faith itself. The net result of their rebellion was a vision of a more thoroughgoing unity in the spiritual life of man than most schemes for establishing an integrated world religion. The cornerstone of this movement of Sufism is brotherhood of man and service to people regardless of their creed, race, or nationality. They opposed any kind of paper idol that created a feud between different religious groups. Their ideology was dedicated to the principle of saving people from the opiate of religion.

It is interesting to note that the Sufi leaders at the beginning

of the movement split in a number of directions on the question
of what attitude to take toward the Islamic Church, which was
both strong and authoritarian. The more orthodox leaders tried
to keep the orthodox Church and its leaders happy, by pretending
that their movement wanted to resurrect tradition and practice
of the Prophet Muhammad. However, they emphasized their reverence and respect to other religions. The liberal approach was
that the purpose of religion is to unite, reconcile, educate,
harmonize, and serve mankind. It is not something abstract that
could be found in a corner of a temple, church, or mosque. It is
an inner feeling between you and your God and your conscience.
It is universal. Forget labels and search your own heart. There
you shall find your God and your guidance. He will help you
to become another Jesus, Moses, or Muhammad. Hafiz, in the
following ode, expresses the feeling of the Sufis:

> Long years my heart had made request of
>     me, a stranger, hopefully
>     (not knowing that itself possessed
>     The Treasure that it sought of me),
> That Jamshid's chalice I should win
> And it would see the world therein.
> That is a pearl by far too rare
> To be contained within the shell
> Of time and space; lost vagrants
> There upon the oceans margin, well
>
> We know it is a vain surmise
> That we should hold so great a prize.
> There was a man that loved God well;
> In every motion of his mind
> God dwelt; and yet he could not tell
> That God was in him, being blind:
> Wherefore as if afar he stood
> And cried, "Have mercy, O my God.
> This problem that had vexed me long
> Last night unto the taverner
> I carried; for my hope was strong
> His judgment sure, that could not err,
> Might awfully solve infallibly
> The riddle that had baffled me.

I saw him standing in his place,
A goblet in his grasp, a smile
Of right good cheer upon his face,
As in the glass he gazed awhile
And seemed to view in vision clear
A hundred truths reflected there.
That friend [Hallaj] who, being raised
Sublime upon the gallows, glorified
The tree that slew him for his crime,
This was the sin for which he died,
That having secrets in his charge,
He told them to the world at large."

So to speak he, adding "But the heart
That has the truth within its hold
And, practicing the rosebud's art,
Conceals a mystery in each fold,
That heart hath well this comment lined
Upon the margin of the mind.

"And if the Holy Ghost descend
In grace and power infinite
His comfort in these days to lend
To them that humbly wait on it,
Theirs too the wondrous works can be
That Jesus wrought in Galilee.

"You twisted coil, you chain of hair
Why doth the lovely Idol spread
To keep me fast and fettered there?
'Ah, Hafiz', so the wise man said,
Tis a mad heart, and needs restraint
That speaks within thee this complaint."[88]

Sufis were disturbed because most of the churches were pre-occupied with their own brand of religion and expressed opposition and distrust of other creeds. There was as much monstrous arrogance, chauvinism, and mistrust among the churches as we can find among big powers. Even Islamic churches forgot the

---

[88] Hafiz, Divan, translated by A. J. Arberry (Cambridge: University Press, 1947), p. 99.

admonition of its founder that "no distinction we make between any religion and to God we are resigned." It succumbed to provincialism by insisting on embracing all other faiths in its own motherly umbrella or higher truth, which in effect relegates the insights of the other religions to the rank of "relative truth," and asserted the supremacy of the specifically Muslim outlook.

The Sufis advocated that there will and should be a frank exchange of ideas among all the religions of the world. Its purpose should be to see that no one culture or tradition enjoys a monopoly of spiritual truth and to stress the transcendent value of personal experience. In other words, if we descend from the mountain peaks of theology, according to Sufis, to the plateau of humanity, all the formulas for the spiritual unification of man converge in perfect harmony.

The Sufis believe in the freedom and integrity of man; they urge the existential self to seek self-transcendence in organic union with mankind and with the mystical or the divine ground of the cosmos. The final values for Sufis are: life, personality, transcendence, and love.

---

Sufism does not claim to be a religion or even the law of human development. It is an invaluable contribution to a world that is torn and tormented by religious, racial, national, and ideological conflicts. From Sufis' contributions we learn that the human spirit is wider than the forces that bear it onward and that to the whole development of man all religions and ideologies are no more than a contribution.

As Christianity and Islam were a revival of the spiritual values of Judaism at the time when corruption, cruelty, and conflicts were dominant in the Persian and the Roman Empires, so the great movement that goes by the name of Sufism was an uprising and reinstatement of men's intellectual and spiritual impluses under the flag of universalism.

Sufi movement survived and influenced the whole culture of Iran and some other parts of the world. It was an earnest return to the simple, natural law and mystic belief of the unity with God. Its strength was its universal acceptance of all religions without distinction and the Neoplatonic idea of things as they were.

For years, researchers, writers, and orientalists have argued about the origin of Sufism. Some contended that Sufism has its roots in Islam; the others believed that it is of Indo-European growth. Both are partly right. Sufism is a combination of all, and nothing more strongly marks the essential unity of man than the affinities we can perceive in an ideology that embraces all the ideas of mankind. Furthermore, no affinity of this kind is more strongly marked than that likeness in the strength and prominence of the moral fiber that knits with some special sort of genius the Persian culture to the genius and history of the living religions.

Sufism, which has been so great a power in Persian culture, was originally the reaction to the corruption, moral indifference, cruelty, and lax rule of conduct at the court of the caliphs and the church in Baghdad. It was a reaction of humanism against tyranny and fanaticism, and it powerfully manifested itself, as was natural, with a people with background and long history in universalism. Eminently Indo-European by its humor, Sufism, by the power it shows, through acknowledging the multiform aspects of the problem of life, and thus smiling at and ridiculing the overcertainty, tenacity, dogmatism, and fanaticism of its time, opened a new page in history of dissent and intellectual integrity. This change manifested itself in the Islamic world, and has had a great part in shaping history of Iran for the last thousand years.

The Sufis, in their writing, attempted to show that no religion has a monopoly on truth, but each religion has much to offer to the rest.

Christianity is unique with its dynamic gospel of unconditional love, which gives it an opportunity to apply itself to social betterment and relief of human misery.

Judaism, during the dark ages, gave to the world the idea of one God and a much needed morality. Islam uniquely emphasizes the unity of God (clouded by seven centuries of the Ottoman Empire, and obscured by the subtleties of Christian theology), and the fraternity of all men regardless of race, color, or creed on a point that other religions were bogged down by some of the secular conceits of their Western culture. "Hinduism and Buddhism excel in seeing the divine ground in its impersonal aspect and they have more advanced techniques for the intuitive understanding of ultimate reality. They achieve more serenity of spirit. They are less tied to pseudo-historical myth, dogmatic literalness in interpretation of religious symbolism and all the sins of pride which follow therefrom. The indigenous Chinese faiths supply more organic communion with the universe than other religions, a communion not only at the level of spirit but at all the levels of human experience, which gives them a cosmic cheerfulness absolutely unique in the history of religions."[89]

Hence, no one church was fully enough developed, according to the Sufis, not to need insight from the others, which cannot be fully assimilated save by self-reconception.

Sufi philosophers, poets, and thinkers were constantly seeking to bring out the essential qualities of man, his intellectual integrity and his social and humanistic responsibility.

Khaja Ansari, a great Sufi leader remarks:

> O man, if you fly you are no better than a fly.
> If you walk on water you are no better than sea urchins,
> If you are true human being your miracle should be making less fortunate people happy.

Sadi, speaking of man's strength and weakness states:

> He is not reputed a man by the wise who contends with a furious elephant; but he is a man in reality who, when angry, speaks no unkind words.

> An ill-mannered youth insulted a Sufi, who patiently bore it saying: "O friend, I am worse than thou speakest of me, for I am more conscious of my faults than thou are."

"I remember" states Sadi, "being pious in my childhood, rising in the middle of the night, to perform my prayer and devotion. One night I was sitting with my father, reciting the Quoran, while

---

[89] Warren Wagar, *The City of Man* (Baltimore: Penguin Books, 1931), pp. 170–72.

the people around us were asleep. I told my father 'not one of these people lifts up his head, to praise and prayer to Almighty. They are as fast asleep as if they were dead.' He replied, 'My dear son! would that thou were also asleep, rather than disparaging people.' "

> The outward state of the Sufi is the patched robes
> It suffices as a display to the face of the people.
> The abandoning of the world, of the lust and of desire,
> Is sanctity; not the abandonment of the robe only.

> Who brings the faults of another to thee and
>     enumerates them will undoubtedly carry their
>     faults to others.

> Be generous to the poor while wealth is in thy hand,
> That fortune and kingdom will leave thy hand.

> O contentment! Make me rich,
> For besides thee no other wealth exists.
> Logman selected the virtue of patience
> Who has no patience, has no wisdom.

> The liberal have no money
> The wealthy have no liberality.

# 7

# The Sufi Literature and
# Universal Brotherhood

A church, a temple or a Kaaba stone,
The Koran or Bible or a martyr's bone,
All these and more my heart can tolerate,
Since my religion now is Love alone.

Abul Ala Maarri

Most of the Persian Sufi poets envisage a universal man, whose
mission is to love his fellowman regardless of race, color, or
creed. They argue that we may belong to any caste, nation or
community: still, we are children of God, impartially loved by
our Father. We may not even believe in a Supreme Being, but
He cares not. What He cares about is our behavior toward our
fellow creatures. His mercy, compassion, love, and grace are
universal and like rays of sunshine on the world, without distinction of friend or foe.

Sadi of Shiraz, commenting on God's love for man, states:

Every leaf of tree, God's grace displays.
Only the sage mind countenances their sacred lays.
Clouds, sun, moon and air,
All work harmoniously.
For thee they always food prepare,

Thou shouldst accept and eat graciously.
For how each day the sun shines and serves,
All praise from us God Almighty deserves.

"God moulded and fashioned us after his image," Sadi continues, "He made us the highest and the noblest of all beings. He gave us mind, conscience and intelligence. He gave us power of control over plants, animals and nature. At the same time he honored us with his attributes: Grace, Kindness, Compassion, Justice, Love and Patience. These attributes distinguish us from animals. With them we are close to God, without them we are worse than animals. Wise men have said that a faithful dog is preferable to a vicious man."

Different methods called religions, philosophies, and doctrines have been adopted by man to satisfy his desire for truth. Though the rituals and practice of the churches and groups appear to be different, their source is one and the same. Prejudice, envy, hatred, and antagonism are man made. They have no place in religion. They are the products of the mind of the men and women with evil design. Unfortunately, they occupy a large portion of the world history.

So many castes and so many creeds,
So many faiths, and so many beliefs,
All have arisen from selfishness of man.
Wise is he who only truth conceives.[1]

Sufi poets liken life in this world to a journey, and the real desire is to reach the goal. The soul is the point whence life starts and where it ends; and all religions at different times have striven to show us how to attain this goal, with joy, love, and grace. "The ways to God are as many as the number of the people on the surface of the world." The experience and joy of each in reaching his destination is different, though all hope to attain the same goal. All the virtuous and wicked, wise and ignorant, rich and poor, move in the same direction and reach the same goal at the end.

---

[1] Inayat Khan, Cit., vol. 5, p. 15.

The purpose of the Sufi, therefore, is to make this path of
life's journey smooth. They hope to reconcile differences and
feuds and to put an end to hatred and prejudices. They also try
to show that a humble sinner, conscious of his shortcomings, is
better than an arrogant, conceited, pious man:

Historians say that in the ancient days,
When Jesus walked on earth (to him be praise!)
There lived a man so bad, so sunk in sin,
That even Satan was ashamed of him;
The Book contained his name so many times,
No room was left to enter all his crimes.
Perished his tree of life, and bore no fruit,
A stupid, cruel, drunken, swinish brute.
Hard by there dwelt a holy devotee,
Known far and wide for strictest piety;
Each was the marvel of the time and place,
The first of wickedness and this of grace.
Jesus (to Him be praise!), I've heard one day
Forth from the desert came and passed that way:
Th' recluse, descending from his casement high,
Fell at His feet with proud humility;
The lost one gazed with wonder at the sight
Like moth bewildered by the candle's light;
Surely one gentle touch had reached his heart,
From Him who came to take the sinner's part!
Shrinking with shame, his conscience stricken sore,
As shrinks a beggar at a rich man's door.
Tears of repentance rolling down his face,
For days and nights polluted with disgrace,
With fear and hope, God's mercy to invoke,
In earnest prayer, with bated breath he spoke:
"My precious life I have I've wasted day by day,
My opportunities I've thrown away;
In vice and wickedness surpassed by none,
No single act of goodness have I done;
Would that like me no mortal e'er might be.
Better by far to die than live like me!
He who in childhood dies is free from blame,
Old age comes not to bow his head with shame,
Forgive my sins, Creator of the world,
Lest I to blackest depths of hell be hurled.

On that side, lo!" the aged sinner cries,
Not daring heavenward to lift his eyes
Repentant, weeping, sunk in deep despair:
"Help of the helpless hear, hear my prayer."
On this, the devotee puffed up with pride
With visage sour from far the sinner eyed.
What brings this ill-starred wretch towards this place,
Dares he to think himself of man's high race?
Headlong to fire eternal he has fallen,
His life to lust's foul whirlwind he had given,
His sin-stained soul what good can show that he
Messiah's company should share with me!
I loathe his fateful countenance, and dread
Lest sin's infection to my bosom spread;
In that great day, when all must present be,
"O God! I pray Thee, raise him not with me."
From the all-glorious God a message came
   to Jesus (ever blessed be His name!):
"The ignorant and the learned both are saved,
Both I accept since both to me have prayed;
The lost one, humbled, with repentant tears
Has cried to me, his cry has reached my ears;
Who helpless lowly seeks, and doth not doubt
The mercy seat, shall never be cast out;
How many wicked deeds I have forgiven,
My boundless mercy brings him to heaven;
And should the devotee on that great day
Think it disgrace in heaven with thee to stay,
Tell him, beware! They take thee not to hell
And him to paradise with God to dwell!"

The sinner's bleeding heart in anguish sighs,
The saint upon his piety relies,
Doth he not know that God resisteth pride,
But takes the low in spirit to His side,
Whose heart is vile, but outside fair to see,
For him hell's gates yawn wide, he wants no key,
Humility in his sight is more meet
Than strict religious forms and self-conceit;
Thy self-esteem but proves how bad thou art,
For egotism with God can have no part,
Boasts not thyself—however swift his pace,

Not every skillful rider wins the race.
Wise men have left for all this saying true,
And Sadi in this tale remindeth you,
The sinner penitent hath less to fear
Than he whose piety is not sincere.[2]

In another poem, Sadi declares that man never can achieve perfection, unless he can forgive his enemies and those who have hurt him. Love is the essence of all religions, mysticisms, and philosophies. The one who has learned secrets of this love fulfills the purpose of religion, ethics, and philosophy, and love is raised above all diversities of faiths and beliefs.

> When the enemy doth throw
>     His lasso,
> As his whim determines, so we
>     must do.
> None has earned, till he has loved,
>     Manly fame,
> E'en as silver pure is proved
>     By the flame
> Never did reformer take
>     Passion's way,
> But that both worlds he must stake
>     In the play.
>
> To his memory I am so
>     Wholly turned,
> That with self my mind is no
>     More concerned.
>
> Thanks to love sincere and whole
>     I confess;
> Love that burned my heart, my soul
>     Doth caress.
>
> Sadi! Poet sweeter page
>     Never writ
> For a present to an age
>     Great wit.

---

[2] Sadi, Bustan, translated by W. C. Mackinnon.

> May thy sugar tongue remain
>    Ever blest,
> That hath taught the world such pain
>    And unrest.[3]

Whatever diversity may exist among people, the reason for creation has been one: to cultivate and prepare the human heart for universal brotherhood, harmony, and love. Man on this earth is full of needs, but among all the different needs, the need of a friend is the greatest. There is no greater misery than hating or being hated.

The whole creation is made for love and friendship. The Sufis believe that the reason for the creation of man is to serve, to help, and to alleviate the suffering of others. Man discovers himself when he starts to share his sorrow, joy, and interests with the rest of mankind who are his friends and collaborators:

> Socrates, the philosopher wise,
> Built him a house of modest size.
> Forthwith about him on every side
> People shouted, and people cried;
> Each of them had a fault to tell
> Of the house he had builded up so well.
> As the philosopher heard them cry
> He laughed aloud, and made reply:
> "Friends, you do wrong to criticize;
> I cannot call your counsel wise.
> Though my small cabin is little worth,
> It is everything I require on earth;
> All I pray is, that it may be
> Filled with friends who are true to me."[4]

---

The Sufis, in elaboration of their doctrine of universalism, state that religion sees things from the aspects of plurality, but mystics regard the world as an all-embracing unity. Both mono-

---

[3] Ibid., translated by A. J. Arberry.
[4] Rashid Yasami, *A Contemporary Poet,* translated by A. J. Arberry, (London: Everyman's Library, 1964), p. 140.

theistic churches and Sufis declare that God is one, but the statement bears a different meaning in each instance. The churches
mean that God is unique in attributes, qualities, and acts, and
he is absolutely different from all other beings. But the Sufis
believe that their God is the one Real Being that underlies all
phenomena. This belief further claims that the whole universe,
including man, is essentially one with God. Man is the crown of
God's universe, though last in the order of creation. Therefore
he has to manifest this unity of the universe in his behavior and
action. As long as he is a captive in the snare of greed for power
and money, it is hard for him to see the beauty of a united mankind, dedicated to the cause of service and assistance. Real humanity is unification of purpose and realization of the fact that
division, whether in the name of religion, nationalism, race, or
color, is a false and deluding dream. The Sufis believe:

> The true mosque in a pure and holy heart
> Is builded: There let all men worship God;
> For there He dwells, not in a mosque of stone.

Hafiz of Shiraz, in the spirit of a universal man declares:

> Love is where the glory falls
> Of thy face—on convent walls
> Or on tavern floors, the same
> Unextinguishable flame.
> When the turbaned anchorite
> Chanteth Allah day and night,
> Church bells ring the call to prayer
> And the Cross of Christ is there.[5]

Sufi poets on many occasions share ideas with free-thinkers,
but they never touch sectarianism. This explains the universal
character of their literature and the fact that they never attached
themselves to any church or Muslim denominations. They always
fought dogmatism and religious demagoguery. "You should never
know anything at all about Sufism until you get completely rid
of pride, prejudice and selfishness."

---

[5] Hafiz, Divvan, translated by Reynold A. Nicholson.

"In proportion," according to Nicholson, "as the Sufi gains more knowledge of God, his religious prejudices are diminished. Sheykh Abd Al-Rahim Ibn Al-Sabbagh, who at first disliked living in upper Egypt, with its large Jewish and Christian population, said in his old age that he would as readily embrace a Jew or Christian as one of his own faith."[6]

While the Sufis acknowledge and approve differences in culture, creed, ritual, and customs, they are absolutely against the ideas and doctrines that in the name of God and Country have caused many wars, much hatred, and enormous damages among nations, communities, and individuals:

> This world and that world are the egg, and
> the bird within it
> Is in darkness and broken-winged and
> scorned and despised.
> Regard unbelief and faith as the white and
> the yolk in this egg,
> Between them, joining and dividing, a barrier
> which they shall not pass.
> When He hath graciously fostered the egg
> under His wing,
> Infidelity and religion disappear: the bird
> of Unity spreads its pinions.[7]
> Not until every mosque beneath the sun
> Lies ruined, will our holy work be done;
> And never will true Muslims appear
> 'Til faith and infidelity are one.

Attar, the mentor of mystic poets and writers, commenting on the state of man on earth, declares:

> We are the Magians of old,
> Islam is not the faith we hold:
> In irreligion is our fame,
> And we have made our creed a shame.

---

[6] Reynold A. Nicholson, *The Mystics of Islam* (London: Routlege & Kegan Paul, Ltd., 1963), p. 89.
[7] Ibid., p. 90.

Now to the tavern we repair
To gamble all substance there,
Now in the monastery cell
We worship with the infidel.

When Satan chances us to see
He doffs his cap respectfully,
For we have lessons to impart
To Satan in the tempter's art.

We were not in such nature made
Of any man to be afraid;
Head and foot, in naked pride
Like sultans o'er the earth we ride.

But we, alas, aweary are
And the road is very far;
We know not by what way to come
Unto the place that is our home.

And therefore we are in despair
How to order our affair
Because, wherever we have sought,
Our minds were utterly distraught.

When shall it come to pass, ah when,
That suddenly, beyond our ken,
We shall succeed to rend this veil
That doth our whole affair conceal?

What veil soever after this
Apparent to our vision is,
With the flame of knowledge true
We shall consume it through and through.

Where at the first in that far place
We came into the world of space,
Our soul by travail in the end
To that perfection shall ascend.

And so shall Attar shattered be
And rapt in sudden ecstasy,
Soar to Godly vision, even
Beyond the veils of earth and heaven.[8]

Maghribi (d. A.D. 1406), a pillar of the Sufi world, describes his idea of the unity and universalism of humanity in the following words:

Ask not the road to the college or the customs
    of the monastery;
Pass by road and custom; ask not about way and road
Adopt the path of poverty and self-effacement
    and be happy;
Look not behind thee, and ask not save of what
    lies before.
When thou steppest forth from the narrow cell
    of the body, ask not save of the Holy precincts
    of the King.
Ask about the delights of poverty and annihilation
    from those who have tasted them;
Ask not of him who is the slave of wealth and rank.[9]

Pir Jamal (d. A.D. 1474), another Sufi mentor, states:

Do not wish ill to anyone, O man of good nature,
Whether they be people of the cell [Christians]
    or of the synagogues,
What a bad place is a bad thought! Hell springs
    from it.
Know that the joys of paradise are from good
    thoughts alone.
Thou art thy own prison. Arise quickly and
    depart!
That is to say self-abandonment is the life
    of the Sufi,
If mysticism consisted in garments of wool and
    felt
Goats and sheep would be the leaders of the Sufis.

---

[8] Attar, translated by A. J. Arberry.
[9] Maghribi, translated by E. G. Browne.

The great Persian philosopher and scientist Abu Ali Sina (d. A.D. 1037) states that a human's function in this world is not hatred, discord, and feud, but to the contrary, the function of the human rational soul is the noblest function of all, for it is itself the noblest of God's creations. Its function consists of reflecting upon good and useful things of this world and meditating upon things of beauty: its gaze being turned toward the higher world; it loves not this lower abode and meaner station. It is waiting for the revelation of truths and to reflect with perfect intuition and unclouded wit upon the perception of subtle ideas, reading with the eye of inner vision the tablet of Divine Mystery and opposing with strenuous devices the causes of vain fancy. It is distinguished from other spirits by the possession of perfect reason and far-reaching, all-embracing thought; its ambition and striving all through life is to help and to purify the sensual impression and to perceive the world of intelligible truths.[10]

Omar Khayyam, in his eloquent words and way, explains:

> Hearts with the light of love illumined well,
> Whether in mosque or synagogue they dwell,
> Have their names written in the Book of Love,
> Unvexed by hopes of heaven or fear of Hell.

> Although the creeds number some seventy-three,
> I hold with none but that love of thee;
> What matter faith, unfaith, obedience, sin?
> Thou art all we need, the rest is vanity.

Hafiz of Shiraz, who is called "The Tongue of the Unseen" (God), in all his odes praises love, unity, brotherhood of man. He is the sworn enemy of hatred, envy, hypocrisy, and religious prejudice:

> Learn from yon orient shell to love thy foe,
> And store with pearls the hand that brings thee woe,
> Free, like yon rock, from base vindictive pride,
> Emblaze with gems the wrist that rends the side:
> Mark, where yon tree rewards the stony shower

---

10 Margaret Smith, *The Sufi Path of Love* (London: Luzac), p. 59.

With fruit nectareous, or the balmy flower;
All nature calls aloud: Shall man do less
Than heal the smiter, and the railer bless.[11]

Come let us pass this pathway o'er
That to the tavern leads;
There waits the wine, and there the door
That every traveller needs.

On that first day, when we did swear
To tipple and to kiss,
I was our oath, that we would fare
No other way but this.

Where Jamshid's crown and royal throne
Go sweeping down the wind;
'Tis little comfort we should moan:
In wine is joy to find.

Because we hope that we may bring
Her waist to our embrace,
Lo, in our life-blood issuing
We linger in this place.

Preacher, our frenzy is complete:
Waste not thy sage advice;—
We stand in the Beloved's Street,
And seek no paradise.

Let Sufis wheel in mystic dance
And shout for ecstasy;
We, too, have our exuberance,
We, too, ecstatics be.

When Hafiz was threatened with excommunication by some religious groups, his answer was:

Go spread thy dainty nets for other wings—
Too high the eagle's nets for thee, my friend.

---

[11] Hafiz, translated by Sir William Jones.

Come vex me not with this eternal sprite;
For old companionship demands its right.
Heed then my counsel, costlier and more rare
Than all the jewels in the casket there.
Yet how to drunkards shall thy face be shown
That holds a mirror to the sun and moon?

Chide not the drunkard, greybeard; place be still;
Or wouldst thou quarrel with the Heavenly Will?
Fearest thou not the fiery breath of me
Shall burn the woolen cassock circling thee?

Pour me the wine of yesternight again
To ease the throbbing of a bankrupt's brain.
Hafiz, thy songs of songs are lovliest;
I swear it, by the scriptures in thy breast.

Zahid, I beg leave my sins alone;
They are not yours—I'll settle for my own.

Each man a sinner is, and may be you,
O white-souled Zahid, are a sinner too.

If I be good—so much the better for me;
If I be bad—so much the worse for—me.

Go be yourself, and your own business mind;
Within the Universe is something kind.

To sinners, Zahid, though you know it not
Behind the veil, behind the veil, God wot,

Maybe the earthly saint is heaven's sinner,
And he who lost on earth in heaven is winner.

It matters not, O most misguided friend,
What little church or chapel we attend,

We all are seeking just the self-same thing,
And love begins and ends our worshipping.

The world to come is good—indeed it is!
But so, believe me, holy one, is this.

Scorn not the joys you have for those you dream—
That shadow of a willow and a stream,

A face of ivory, a breast of myrrh,
And someone singing—Zahid, O beware.

Lest you let slip realities like these
For theologic unrealities.

If you are kind, thank God that it is so;
If you are good—don't let your neighbors know.

But my poor poet Hafiz, as for you,
What on the Day of Judgment will you do!
Knock softly with a wine-cup on the door,
And be assured that they will let you through.

> Thrice holy night! O hallowed rising moon!
> O waiting trees! O stars that burn so bright!
> O radiant planet, was it yours the boon?
> This is the night of my first wondering look
> Into her eyes, the night she came to me
> Right out of heaven—like the holy book;
> O bright beginning of felicity,
> This is the night.

> Tonight the Mussalman is at his prayers;
> Spinning in solemn jury circle-wise,
> The dervish chants, for holy church declares
> The Quoran like a star shot from the skies—
> This very night.

> I also shall observe the sacred rites:
>    Bent low before her on adoring knees,
> In a strong circle of my faithful love
> I'll keep her safe as gold as sanctuaries.
> O river singing to the stars above
>    O Night of Nights!

> Ah! Zahid, can you dream I will give up
>    A love like this—for pious platitude,
> Or cease to crush the grape into the cup!
> I, Sufi, may be wrong, you may be right—

> Hafiz must tread his self-appointed way
>     And on her red lips find his heavenly food.
> If you must talk, O talk some other day—
>     But not to-night.

> When thus I sit with roses in my breast,
> Wine in my hand, and the Beloved Kind;
> I ask no more—the world can take the rest
>     Even the Sultan's self is, to my mind,
> On such a planetary night as this,
>     Compared with me a veritable slave.[12]

Whatever mystical meanings may lie beneath, the poems of Hafiz are loved and admired for their sweetness, the fullness of their humanity and liberalism.

Compared with his infinite variety, Omar Khayyam seems doctrinaire—for Hafiz, while he shares Omar's contempt for religious hypocrisy, and likewise sings the philosophy of pleasure, is not so seriously concerned in such criticism of life as Omar is, but is occupied rather with living itself. . . . The philosophy of Hafiz is a matter of daily wisdom, to act on rather than to preach—the tacit philosophy of a man of the world who was a poet as well. Omar has something of the spirit of the reformer, and the burden of the mystery lies heavy upon him. Hafiz, however, is less serious-minded. He is, as we say, more instinctively a pagan, and his poetry has thus a "human interest" that Omar lacks.[13]

> Life is not worth the trouble; the whole sky,
> With all its pomp and pageantry of stars,
> Was never worth the heaving of a sigh.
> Yea! even all this goodly realm of Mars,
> With Shiraz as the jewel in its crown,
> Would find no merchant fool enough to buy
> If Shiraz were not the Beloved's town.
> Go sell your clouted prayer-coat if you can,
> And see if any vintner counts it worth

---

[12] Richard Le Gallienne, *Odes From the Divan of Hafiz* (London: Duckworth & Co., 1905), pp. 21, 25, 28.

[13] Ibid., pp. XXVI, XXVII.

A single cup of valuable wine,
Drawn from the musty cellars of old earth;
If so, you'll get more than I get for mine.

Yea! a prayer-carpet made in Turkistan,
Most excellent in colour and design
For sale I offered in the vintner's street:
"All colours at once! O woven and dyed deceit!
For you exchange this Cup of honest red!
Never!" the Abbot of the wine-house said.

Dangers and hardships of life's troubled sea,
At first they seemed to me a little thing;
But ah! that weary old pearl-fishery
Hath more of perils nowdays than pearls;
'Tis not worthwhile—I let the others drown.

Ye! Who would even choose to be a king,
And wear a royal crown upon his head,
If he must lose his head to wear his crown,
No, Hafiz, 'tis a small world and a vile,
Not worth a second thought when all is said;
What if my heart low down has whispered—
"Even the well-beloved is not worth while."[14]

Hafiz's poetry is not only humanistic but lyrical and continually engages our interest by glimpses of a personal human drama. It possesses compassion, kindness, magnanimity, and frankness, as well as lyrical music, and it is a mirror of that tumultuous and troublesome world. Hafiz compares his work to a "conserve of roses," but it is more accurate to say that "human breadth, vivid passion, pervasive humor, high spirits and an intense love of nature" are qualities that make Hafiz's poetry dear to its readers:

The Abbot of the Wine-house for thy friend,
Thou shalt have peace and pleasure without end;
So gracious He to all our vinous race,
In common gratitude we all abase

---

[14] Ibid., pp. 69, 70.

Our heads before Him on the tavern floor—
It were superfluous to praise Him more.
All the old fables men have ever told
Of Heaven's High Mansion builded all of gold
Pointed to this our palace of wine,
Home of the ruddy daughter of the grape.
Misers for gold and silver sourly scrape,
But we of the generous heart spend the red wine—
Misers and spendthrifts we of the red wine.
The wine-house garden is so fair a place,
So fresh the running stream, so soft the air,
I am content to sit a lifetime there.

O'er each man's brow God ran his pen of Fate;
We read the writing when it is too late.
With hidden treasure lurks the hidden snake.
Honor no man for birth, but his own sake;

Yea, honor him according to his deeds.
Whoso with understanding Hafiz reads
Knows that he striveth ever, night and day,
After the good deed and the perfect way.

I hug the wine-jar thus, and folk believe,
Seeing me bent in such studious way,
I keep the blesses Quoran up my sleeve.
With all the smoulder of hypocrisy,
Some day I should not be surprised at all
If this old lying garment should take fire
And publicity proclaim me for a liar;
Surely it could not burn too fast for me—
The tavern-keeper takes no pay in prayers.

You who against the cup admonish us,
Thus making war on a divine decree,
Your very visage, dour and dolorous,
The pain of your own abstinence declares;
You do without—but how reluctantly!

Wine to the pure in heart is heart's delight,
Because its ruby no impression takes—
Saving the very face sober truth.

As I talk on, as yonder candle bright,
I cannot keep from smiling 'mid my tears
To think of all this music my tongue makes,
This wasted eloquence she never hears.
Good Sufi, cease—you weary me in sooth!
You bid me take my eyes from off her face!
Deafen no more already deafened ears—
Take your tongue rather to some other place.

Once more red wine hath turned my willing head,
    Once again completely vanquished me!
Turned my old yellow cheek rosy red—
    Blessings, red wine, on thee!

Blessings upon the hand, long since with God,
    That plucked the first grape from the primal vine,
And blest his feet that first the wine-press trod
    True friend he was of mine.

And fate has written "lover" on the brow,
    Accept thy doom; resistance is in vain;
Best to the tragic signature to brow—
    Fate rubs not out again.

Boast not of wisdom: hast thou ever thought
    That Aristotle must give back his mind
To death at last, even as the most untaught
    And savage of mankind.

Zahid, scold not, though fallen in arrear
    Our pious dues—we'll settle them some day;
If is not, small sum—give us another year;
    God's debts are hard to pay.

This is the way to live—that when thou diest
    No one believes that thou art really dead;
Hafiz, thy song the power of death defied
    As long as rose is red.

Hafiz is drunk in many different ways—
Drunk with the Infinite, drunk with the Divine,
With music drunk, and many a lovely face;
    Also he is drunk—with wine.

Talk to me not about the Book of Sin,
   For friend, to tell the truth,
That is the book I would be written in—
   It is so full of youth.

And mark me friend, when on the Judgment Day
   The black book and the white
Are Angel-opened there in Allah's sight,
   For all to read what's writ;

Just watch how lonely the white book will be!
   But the black book, wherein is writ my name,—
   My name, my shame, my fame,—
With busy readers all besieged you'll see,
   Yea, almost thumbed away—
   So interesting it.

And as for this, my fatal love of wine,
   Believe me, friend, it is no fault of mine—
'Tis fate, just fate; and surely you don't think
   I fear a God that destined me to drink?

This life of Hafiz was the gift of God—
To God some day I'll give it back again;
Ah! Have no fear! When Hafiz meets his God,
   I know He will not call it lived in vain.[15]

Superficial religion has no credit with Hafiz. Mankind in reality is man-honest, frank, universal, and compassionate. He needs no intermediary to get to heaven or to be on good terms with his Creator. By reality, Hafiz means simple, natural, and helpful living, the possession and employment of the qualities naturally appertaining to the order to which the human race belongs. The final object in life is a search for truth. And truth is that mankind should speak aright, act aright, and think aright, or in other words become wise and helpful.

The object of life, according to Hafiz, is threefold: first, that man may not become like the brute; secondly, that he may be

---

[15] Ibid., pp. 75–77.

adorned with grace, piety, gentleness, and avoid conflict and discord; thirdly, that he may dedicate his life to service of his fellowmen and strive to alleviate human suffering with love and kindness:

Preacher, it is all in vain you preach to me,
   Nor business of anyone's but mine.
Where I have sinned and what may and will be,
   I ponder too on subtleties divine—
Pray solve me this: how Allah out of naught
   The waist of my Beloved made so fine
That it exists but in the lover's thought,
   Nor can be apprehended of the eye,
A metaphysic fancy of the mind—
   Solve me this riddle, preacher, how and why.

Again, you promise, when we leave behind
   This jasmined earth, its roses and its dew,
Eight paradises up there in the sky;
   I' faith, it makes a man in haste to die
To think of living after death with you!
   Listen! one corner of the earth with her
Is more to me than all the stars on high;
   Down here's my heaven, though yours may be up there!

What if to ruin all my life has gone?
   Upon that very ruin do I rear
   This building of my dream, and very fair
Is it to dwell in and to look upon—
   This tavern-temple of the thought of Her.
And, if to you my fate should seem unkind,
   Unjust my love, and ofttimes harsh to me,
It is enough that she it was designed
   This exquisite anguish of my destiny.[16]

Love is a church where all religions meet,
Islam or Christ, or tavern, it is one;
Thy face of every system is the sun—
Sun that shines in the Beloved's street.

---

[16] Ibid., pp. 28, 29.

Where love is there is no need of convent bell,
And holy living needs no holy frocks;
Time ticks not to your monastery clocks;
Where Goodness is there God must be as well.

My friend! Ah yes, fill all the sky with foes,
Against me be heaven and earth and hell allied,
Darken the earth with armies, thick as the rose—
I care not if my friend is on my side.

After a well-spent life comes paradise,
With palaces fair painted on the skies;
We topers know a better heaven than this:
The tavern, to our wayward thinking, is
    Heaven enough.

Upon the margin of the stream we sit
And watch the world with a contented eye;
The stream glides onward and ever, and so it
    As surely passes by.

Brief joy, long paid, is all the world can give;
Pour on the stream and learn this lesson rough:
If you the gain, we find the loss, to live
    More than enough.

To sit with the Beloved, who could more
    Ask of a world so very sad as this—
Yea, even could a happier world give more?
    Ah, drive me not, Beloved from thy door
    With harsh rebuff;

For knowest thou not thy doorstep is my home?
    Nor send me to some distant realm of bliss—
No knowledge crave I of the world to come,
    For never I of this old world that is
    Can have enough.[17]

---

[17] Ibid., pp. 45–46.

Sufis believe that the cause of conflict and corruption in this world is selfishness and greed. In order that man should meet his responsibility and fulfill his mission of humanity, he has to renounce what separates him from his Creator and his fellow-creatures. Renunciation is of two kinds: external and internal. The former is the renunciation of worldly wealth and greed; the latter is the renunciation of desires. Everything that separates us from humanity and causes prejudice and hatred must be renounced. Wealth and power should be used to remedy the maladies of our society, otherwise they are great hindrances. Even too much prayer and fasting could be detrimental to our work and performance. "The only worship," according to Sadi, "is involvement and service to those who need our help."

Man must renounce idolatry, if he desires to remain free. Most people invent some kind of idol that they worship; with one it is wealth and power; with another prayer and fasting. When a man spends all of his time in accumulating gold or in prayer, his gold or his prayer-carpet becomes his idol. Renunciation is the characteristic mark of the liberated wise man.

The fleeting phantoms you admire today
Will soon at Heaven's behest be swept away.[18]

When I saw with eyes discerning that this world's
   the home of woe,
And that o'er the best and noblest death his cerement
   doth throw,
And that fate, false friend, to cheat me and to rob
   me did propose;
Then from off ambition's sick-bed wholly cured, thank God,
   I rose;
To the drug-shop of repentence hastened and did there beseech
Tonic medicine to give me strength to practise what I preach.
Therefore, now this tongue, which lately sang the praise
   of earthly kings,
Unto God, the King eternal, humble praise as tribute brings.
Five yards of wool or cotton are sufficient to contain
A body free from vain desires, a calm untroubled brain.

---

18 Jami (d. 1492).

Long while the praise and service of princes was my care;
To God I now will offer my service and prayer.[19]

If thou wish to become a pilgrim on the path of love and service, the first step is humility and dedication. Next comes renunciation.

Those who desire worldly position and possession for their
own selfish interests are always haunted by sorrow and misery.
Those who desire paradise are businessmen making a deal with
God. But those who desire God without rewards in this or the
next world have reached the path of humanity and glory.

> The heart inquired of soul, what is the beginning of the busi-
> ness of a Sufi? What is its end? And what is the reward?

> The soul answered: the beginning of the Sufi path is abandon-
> ing of selfishness, greed and hatred. Its price is faithfulness.
> Its reward is peace of mind and eternal happiness.[20]

The heart of the Sufi's dogma of universalism is that the
souls of men differ in degree but not at all in kind. They are
parts of that Divine Spirit of God which dominates the universe.
He alone is perfect, benevolent, compassionate, and absolute
Truth. His love alone is real and genuine and the cause of joy
and happiness of mankind.

Sufism regards all religions and philosophical ideas "as more
or less perfect or imperfect shadowings of the great central Truth
which it seeks fully to comprehend and consequently recognizes
all of them as food in proportion to the measure of truth which
they contain."

> The world is baffled in its search for Thee!
> Wealth cannot find Thee, no, nor poverty:
>     All speak of Thee, but none have ears to hear,
>     Thou'rt near to all, but none have eyes to see.

---

19 Masud-i-sad, Salman translated by E. G. Browne, *Literary History of Persia,*
   vol. 2 (London: T. Fisher, 1906), p. 325.
20 Anari of Herold (d. 1090).

The world's a body and the "Truth" its soul,
The angels are its senses, they control
    Its limbs—the creatures, elements and spheres;
All seem to be, one only is the whole.[21]

Sufism is a word and an idea uniting many divergent meanings and different sects and religions. The Sufis are not a sect. They have no dogmatic system except universal brotherhood and love. The essence of Sufism is best displayed in pantheistic and speculative terms rather than ascetic or devotional.

"Sufism is not a system composed of rules or sciences but a moral disposition; i.e., if it were a rule, it could be made one's own by strenuous exertion, and if it were a science, it could be acquired by instruction; but on the contrary it is a disposition. Sufism is freedom and generosity and absence of self-constraint."[22] Sufism is the message of love, brotherhood, and peace. States L. Massignon,

It is, thanks to its mysticism, that Islam is a religion which is international and universal. It has given new life to Islam, has been a method of whole-hearted self-examination, turning to account *ab intera* all the events of life, good fortune and bad; making those who pursued it to the end, into physicians able to give help to others who were unfortunate.

Sufism is a treatment which the physician has first tried on himself in order to benefit others.

Moreover, the social importance of Islamic mysticism comes from its supposed remedial value. Have its teachers, as they maintain, been able in their inner life to draw upon the means of "healing the sickness of heart", of dressing the wounds of a community injured by the errors of the unworthy members? Our only means of making sure that the Islamic mystics, by their efforts, attained their goal, is to examine the social consequences: the values and effectiveness of their rule of life as a cure for the ills of society . . . the lasting force of Islamic mysticism . . . lay in the superhuman desire of sacrifice for

---

[21] Omar Khayyam, translated by E. H. Whinfield.
[22] Nicholson, *Mystics of Islam*, p. 26.

one's fellows, in the transcendent ecstasy of the martyr, expressed by Hallaj: "Forgive them, but do not forgive me."[23]

Fools buy false coins because they are like the true.
If in the world no genuine minted coin were
current, how would forgers pass the false?
Falsehood were nothing unless truth were there,
To make it specious. 'Tis the love of right lures
men to wrong. Let poison but be mited with sugar,
they will cram it into their mouths. Oh, cry not
that all creeds are vain! Some scent of truth
they have, else they would not beguile. Say not,
"How utterly fantastical!"
No fancy in the world is all untrue,
Amongst the crowd of dervishes hides one,
One true Dervish. Search well and thou wilt find![24]

Cheer one sad heart; thy loving deed will be
More than a thousand temples built by thee.
One free man whom thy kindness hath enslaved
Outweighs by far a thousand slaves set free.[25]

---

[23] Smith, *Sufi Path of Love*, pp. 19, 20.
[24] Rumi, translated by R. A. Nicholson.
[25] Nasrollah S. Fatemi, Faramarz S. Fatemi, and Fariborz S. Fatemi, *Sufism: Message of Brotherhood, Harmony, and Hope* (South Brunswick and New York: A. S. Barnes and Co., Inc., 1976), p. 64.

# 8

## Sufism and the Idea of Pantheism

I was a Hidden Treasure, and I desired to be known, therefore,
I created the Universe that I might be known.

—The Koran

I never saw anything without seeing God therein.

—Muhammad Wassi

Most Western orientalists assert that Sufism is a pantheistic
doctrine borrowed from the Greeks. Reynold Nicholson, referring
to this assertion, states that the Sufi ascetic stage belongs to the
Arab race. But hand in hand with the Persian revival under "the
Abbasids came a new current of ideas. Speculation takes a bolder
flight and essays to reconcile the creature with his creator, to
bridge the chasm between the finite and the infinite." It is at
this stage that many diverse ideas from the East and West received a friendly welcome among the Sufi thinkers and poets.

Dhu'l Nun (b. A.D. 859) introduced the doctrine of ecstasies
and mystical stages. Sini Sagati (b. A.D. 880) originated the
idea of unification and presence of God in everything.

Jami, in his book *Nafakhatu l Uns*, states that Dhu'l Nun is
not only the founder of the Sufi sect, but that all the theories and
doctrines of Sufism are derived from and attributed to him.

There were other "pillars" before him, but Dhu'l Nun was first to interpret symbolic expressions and to lecture on Sufism.

In A.D. 922, Mansur Hallaj asserted that all things are God or the All is God. He further claimed that man is essentially divine. God created Adam in his own image. He projected from Himself that image of His eternal love, that He might behold Himself as in a mirror. Hence He made angels worship Adam in whom, as in Jesus, He became incarnate:[1]

> Glory to Him who revealed in His humanity [i.e., in Adam] the secret of His radiant divinity, and then appeared to His creatures visibly in the shape of one who ate and drank [Jesus].

Since the humanity (*Nasut*) of God comprises the whole bodily and spiritual nature of man, the divinity (*Lahut*) of God cannot unite with that nature except by means of an incarnation or infusion (*hulul*) of the Divine Spirit, such as takes place when the human spirit enters the body. This idea encourages Hallaj to say: *"ana'l Hagg,"* "I am God."

> Thy spirit is mingled in my spirit even as it
>     is mingled with pure water.
> When anything touches thee, it touches me.
> Lo, in every case Thou art I.
>
> I am He whom I love, and He whom I love is I;
> We are two spirits dwelling in one body.
> If thou seest me, thou seest Him,
> And if thou seest Him, thou seest both.[2]

Hallaj was barbarously executed. "But," according to Nicholson, "the word had been spoken and henceforth Sufism is frankly pantheistic."

The rapid expansion of the Islamic empire brought Sufism in contact with other cultures. Persian, Hindu, and Greek philosophy were introduced. The works of many writers, poets, and

---

[1] Koran 2:32.
[2] Louis Massignon, *Kital sl-Tawasin* (Paris: 1913), pp. 134–41.

philosophers appeared in Arabic. Sufism, moreover, had its organized medicants who traveled to every part of the Eastern world. Often these wanderers were men of active and ingenious minds. In this way, as we have noticed in the previous chapters, Zoroastrian, Manichaean, Buddhist, Jewish, Greek, and Christian ideas were added to the Islamic tradition and philosophy. "The idea of emanation," states Nicholson, "or rather the particular form of it exhibited in Sufism proceeded, if we are not mistaken, from the Neoplatonic mind." Sufi metaphysics—naturally the product of mature speculation—are cast throughout in the mold that Alexandria aptly contrived to satisfy once, the despairing credulity and devotional enthusiasm of the time. This resemblance, extending also to practical ethics, would be still more striking, were it not disguised by a total contrast of expression. What Plotinus states tersely and boldly, "*Jalal ud Din*," flows into an obscure allegory: "He implies things, but seldom utters them. He is so vague, fanciful and allusive, that the depth of his acquaintance with Greek and Arabian philosophy cannot be definitely fixed."[3]

However, the Persian terminology for God (*Hama Oust*), "All is He," and the Arabic expression *Whadtat al Wujud*, "the unity of being," fairly interpret some connection with the aim of Plotinus to achieve perfect union with God.

The question is asked: "Does the Koran offer a basis for any type of pantheism?" The Koran's God is different from his creatures. The universe has a real existence apart from its Creator. The creation of the universe is a reality. It came from nothing and its existence depends upon God, who ordered it into creation, and its future existence depends upon God.

The Sufis took the theistic ideas of the Koran and turned them into a type of pantheism through interpretation of different verses. "The transcendent God who, at first as it were, standing outside of his creation, supports it and knows it, and manages it, comes nearer and nearer to man than his own jugular vein, identifies himself with some of his actions then passes into the light of heaven and the earth, and finally enters utter immanence, where

---

[3] R. A. Nicholson, *Divani Shamsi Tabriz* (Cambridge: University Press, 1898), pp. XXX and XXXII.

he is the beginning and the end. He is the outward and He is the Inward, and everything passes and only the Being of the Lord of Glory and Beneficence abides."

The following verses are cited by the Sufis to prove the idea of pantheism in the Koran:

Whithersoever ye turn, there is the face of God![4]

For we are closer to him than his jugular vein.[5]

God stands between man and his heart.[6]

God is the light of the Heavens and the earth.[7]

He is the First and the Last, the Evident and the Immanent.[8]

My Lord is close to me ready to answer.[9]

I am indeed close to them.[10]

Everything that exists will perish except His face.[11]

Relying on these verses from the Koran and their knowledge of the Greek philosophy, the Sufis cautiously traveled between monotheism and pantheism.

The early Sufis strived to move away from the world and get closer to God. This movement was first actuated by fear and then dominated by love and gnosis. Later Bayazid Bastami came out with the idea of the ultimate identification of the worshiper and the worshiped, or the lover and the beloved. With him we find the first expression of the concept of annihilation in God that plays such an important part in later Sufism. Long before Hallaj, Bayazid asserted that God was in everything. Furthermore, he

---

[4] Koran 2:115.
[5] Koran 1:16.
[6] Koran 8:24.
[7] Koran 24:35.
[8] Koran 62:3.
[9] Koran 11:61.
[10] Koran 2:186.
[11] Koran 28:88.

identified himself with God, saying: "Verily, I am God, so worship me." In Bayazid, also, we find ecstasy as a form of divine contact, standing higher than morality, worship, and knowledge. Simple resignation and trust in God did not interest him. He told the ascetics: "Leave aside thy resignation." He was blamed for not following rituals and church services. To that he answered that the true knowledge of God should annihilate individuality of the knower, who sees the face of his Friend all the time. He also declared: "I went from God to God until they cried out from me within me, 'O Thou I', at this state I was annihilated in God."

I am like a fathomless ocean identified with God.

Whoever is annihilated in God and attains to the reality of everything, he becomes all Truth, if he is not there, it is only God that sees Himself.

It was during the golden era of Islam (ninth and tenth centuries) that Sufi asceticism passed into speculation on the relation of the finite and the infinite and the worship of God passed into love of a God Who is All in All.
Jami (1492) declares:

> Thou movest under all the forms of truth,
> Under the forms of all created things:
> Look where I will, still nothing I discern
> But there in all the universe.

The Absolute Beauty is the Divine Majesty endued with the attributes of power and bounty. Every beauty and perfection manifested in the theatre of the various grades of beings is a ray of His perfect beauty reflected therein. Whosoever is wise derives his wisdom from the Divine Wisdom. Wherever intelligence is found it is the fruit of the Divine Intelligence.[12]

Much of the Persian Sufi poetry considers the Infinite Being as one ocean of existence from which the waves of the phenomenon

---

[12] Jami, translated by E. H. Whinfield.

arise only to sink back again into it and their being and not being are identical. In this way, they eliminate personal relations within the absolute. Farid Ud Din Attar employs the following analogies for the illustration of the relation of unity to multiplicity:

Water is water in the boundless oceans; in
the jug too it is the same water.

For the wise men, there is no power outside
the most glorious God.

All multiplicity is the repetition of unity.

Thou art more obvious than all that appears!

In the universe if you see even a thousand phenomena, to the men of faith they are one, like the book with separate parts when you turn its leaves and look, it is one [in meaning].

And as His essence all the world pervades,
Naught in creation is, save this alone,
Upon the water has He fixed His throne,
This earth suspended in the starry space,
Yet what are seas and what is air? For all
Is God, and but a talisman are heaven and earth
To veil Divinity. For Heaven and earth,
Did He not permeate them, were but names.
Know then, that both this visible world and that
Which unseen is, alike are God Himself,
Naught is, save God; and all that is, is God.
And yet alas! by low Jew is He seen,
Blind are men's eyes, though all resplendent shines
The world by Deity's own light illumined,
O Thou whom man perceiveth not, although
To him Thou deignest to make known Thyself;
Thou all creation art, all we behold, but Thou,
The soul within the body lies concealed,
And Thou dost hide Thyself within the soul,

O soul in Soul! myst'ry in myst'ry hid!
Before all wert Thou, and art more than all![13]

Emerson sums up the Sufi ideas of love, where he states:

Beholding in many souls the traits of the divine beauty,
and separating in each soul that which is divine from the taint
which it has contracted in the world, the lover ascends to the
highest beauty, to the love and knowledge of the Divinity, by
steps on this ladder of created souls.

"Man's love," says Hujwire, "is a quality which manifests
itself, in the heart of the pious believer, in the form of veneration
and magnification, so that he seeks to satisfy his Beloved and
becomes impatient and restless in his desire for vision of Him,
and cannot rest with any except Him, and grows familiar with
the recollection of Him, and abjures the recollection of everything
besides."

Rumi teaches that Love is "the astrolabe of heavenly mysteries, inspires all religion worthy of the name, and brings with
it, not reasoned belief, but the intense conviction arising from
immediate intuition."

O my Soul I searched from end to end:
I saw in thee naught save the Beloved;
Call me not infidel, O my Soul, if I say
that thou thyself art He.

In his book *Lives of the Saints,* Attar gives the description and
teaching of others and reflects his own subjective bias toward
Greek pantheism. However, to strike

a compromise between theism that views creation as existing
outside God, and utter pantheism that identifies everything
with God, the Sufis developed another doctrine with the help
of the Greek conception of Being and non-Being, attaining a
kind of negative reality to the latter. So we have pure Being
and Being mixed with non-Being. This was nothing but matter

---

[13] Attar, translated by L. M. Garnett. (Attar was born in A.D. 1120. He is considered among the great Sufi poets.)

and form of Aristotle, or the idea of Plato that is real Being impressing itself upon or realizing itself through matter, which is nothing but utter passivity or possibility of the receptivity of form. So all that we call the Universe is a mixture of Being and non-Being. Truth and goodness and beauty are the attributes of Being which exist in their perfection only in the pure Being, but in the world they are mixed with their opposites that have only a negative existence. This Greek conception was taken up by Sufism in order to escape the charge of pantheism, without giving up their basic formula that real Being is only one and belongs to God only. The rank of things in the scale of life is proportionate to their participation in real Being and their imperfections are due to the element of non-Being. This hypothesis termed Wahdat Al-Shuhud (The unity of manifestation) was opposed to Wahdat Al-Wujud (Unity of Being) which accepted in its entirety cuts at the root of all morality and positive religion and justifies the witty remark of William James that monoism is a moral holiday.[14]

The first great Sufi mystic who is considered pantheistic is Ibn Al Arabi (b. 1240). But he too made so many compromises with positive religion that the controversy of centuries has not been able to pronounce a judgment upon him. This difficulty also is experienced by every other Sufi poet when he tries to explain his view of God. "That real Being belongs to God only, and only He really exists." If this doctrine is identical with pantheism, then there is no mistake in pronouncing Sufism in general as pantheistic.

One must also remember that Sufism is a phenomenon of intense religious experience based on emotion rather than on logic. But when we study closely the essential characteristics of Sufi pantheism we realize how fundamentally it differs from all forms of logical conception of Western pantheism. Hence, it is clear that the pantheism of the Sufis must not be confounded with European pantheism of the present day.

Ibn Al Arabi states:

The creator who is declared to be incomparable is the crea-

---

14 Abdul Hakim Khalifa, *The Metaphysics of Rumi* (Lahore, Pakistan: Institute of Islamic Culture, 1965), pp. 150–52.

tures who are compared with Him—by reason of His manifestation Himself in their forms—albeit the creatures have
been distinguished from the Creator. The Creator is the creature, and the creature is the Creator: all this proceeds from
the essence; nay, He is the one essence and the many [indi-
vidualized] essences. The essence is in reality Nature. The
world of Nature is many forms in one mirror; nay, one form
in different mirrors. Bewilderment arises from the difference
of view, but those who perceive the truth of what I have stated
are not bewildered.[15]

In the Beatific Vision God manifests himself to the elect in a
general epiphany which, nevertheless, assumes various forms
corresponding to the mental conceptions of God formed by the
faithful on earth. There is, then, one single epiphany, which
is multiple only by reason of the difference of forms by which
it is received. The vision impregnates the elect with Divine
Light, each experiencing the vision according to the knowledge
of the Divine dogma, or dogmas, gained by him on earth.

Whoso knows himself knows his Lord.
I know the Lord by the Lord, without doubt or wavering. My
essence is His essence in truth, without defect or flaw. There
is no becoming between these two and my soul it is which
manifests that secret.

And since I knew myself without blending or mixture, I attained to Union with my Beloved, without far or near.

"Those who adore God in the skin," says Arabi; "behold
the sun, and those who adore Him in living things see a living
thing, and those who adore Him as a Being unique and un-
paralleled see that which has no like.

"Do not attach yourself to any particular creed exclusively,
so that you disbelieve in all the rest, otherwise, you will lose
much good, nay, you will fail to recognise the real truth of the
matter. God the Omnipotent and Omnipresent, is not limited
by any one creed, for he says in the Quoran, 'Wheresoever ye
turn, there is the face of Allah!' Every one praises what he

15 Ibn Al Arabi, translated by Reynold Nicholson.

believes; his God is his own Creature, and in praising it he praises himself. Consequently he blames the beliefs of others, which he would not do if he were just, but his dislike is based on ignorance."

Junaid says: "The water takes its colour from the vessel containing it."

Hafiz of Shiraz, referring to God's presence everywhere declares:

> Love is where the glory falls
> of Thy face—on convent walls
> or on tavern floors, the same
> unextinguishable flame.

When Arabi was accused of being affected by the ideas of pagan Greeks, he was obliged to write a commentary on some of his poetry, stating that they were not anti-Islam or designed to celebrate the beauty of his mistress.[16]

Sufis, according to Arabi, cannot impart their feelings and spiritual experience to other men. They can only indicate them symbolically to those who see God in everything and are earnest to abandon hatred, envy, and selfishness. Each seeker of the Truth goes through different experience, depending on his temperament and character.

"But," continues Arabi, "no religion is more sublime than a religion of love and seeing God in every place. Love is the essence of all creeds; the true mystic welcomes it whatever guise it may assume."

Rumi, in expressing his idea of Sufi pantheism, declares: "God is the cupbearer, the cup and the wine. He knows what manner of love is mine."

Many Sufi poets consider this universe the mirror of God, the mirror in which He sees Himself:

---

[16] Arabi, on a voyage to Mecca, met an enchanting Persian damsel and fell in love with her. To attract her attention he composed a number of love songs named "An Expression of the Feeling of Longing." When his opponents accused him of pagan tendencies he wrote a commentary interpreting his love songs in a mystical experience.

Look not askance, the Holy one will ever be the same,
The God of all, though oft invoked by many a
different name.

In the words of the Sufi philosopher Shihab ud Din Suhrawardi, born in 1153, we find a tendency to unite the major trends
of pre-Islamic theosophical tradition of old Iran, ancient Egypt,
and the Greek philosophers. He summarizes his theory in the
following words:

> The Essence of the First Absolute Light, God gives constant
> illumination, whereby it is manifested and it brings all things
> into existence, giving life to them by its rays. Everything in
> the world is derived from the Light of His Essence and all
> beauty and perfection are the gift of His bounty, and to attain
> fully to this illumination is salvation.[17]

During Suhrawardi's travel in Islamic countries of the Middle
East, he was imprisoned in Aleppo, where he died in prison at the
age of thirty-eight. He was given the title of Al Magtoul, "the
murdered man."

Suhrawardi is also called "the Master of the Philosophy of
Illumination." His theories concerning this subject are presented
in fifty Persian and Arabic books and tracts. They show influences
and criticism of the Iranian, Hellenistic, and ancient Oriental
philosophy and traditions.

The following quotation represents Suhrawardi's theory of
pantheism:

> Some of my friends asked me, saying, "Tell us the quality of
> the king's majesty and the description of His beauty and
> splendour." Though I am not able to achieve this, yet I will
> say something brief. Know, that whenever ye picture a beau-
> tiful thing in your thoughts unadulterated with any ugliness,
> or a perfect thing which is hedged about by no imperfection,
> there you will find Him. For all beauties are really His: now
> He is the loveliness of every lovely face, now the generosity

---

17 Hussein Nasr, *Three Muslim Sages*, (Cambridge: University Press, 1963), p. 69.

of every open hand. Whoever does His Service, the same finds eternal happiness; but he that turns away from Him has lost both this world and the next.[18]

He who attains tranquility knows about the minds of men, and sees his God in everything. The man reaches such a stage that whenever he likes, he gives up the body and visits the Divine Majesty all over the world.

What is Sufism? Its beginning is facing God and as regards the end, it has no end.

There is no He and I but me, that is the stage of unity.

God is everywhere and in everything.


Rumi in eloquent words expresses the Sufi's belief about monoism and pantheism:

> I have put duality away, I have seen that the two worlds
>    are one;
> One I seek, One I know, One I see, One I call.
> He is the first, He is the last, He is the outward,
>    He is the inward;
> I know none other except He and "He alone".
> I am intoxicated with love's cup, the two worlds have
>    passed out of my ken;
> I have no business save carouse and revelry.
>
> No joy have I found in the two worlds apart from
>    Thee, Beloved.
> Many wonders I have seen. I have not seen a wonder
>    like Thee.[19]


"In whatever we may set our foot," says Rumi, "we are always, Lord, within Thy resort. In whatever place or corner we may entrench ourselves, we are always near to Thee. Per-

18 Suhrawardi, translated by A. J. Arberry.
19 Rumi, *Divvan Shamsi Tabriz*, translated by R. Nicholson.

haps, we say, there is a path which leads elsewhere, and yet, let our pathway be whatever it will, it invariably leads to Thee."[20]


The real workman is hidden in His workshop.
Go you into that workshop and see him face to face.
Inasmuch as over that Workman His work spreads a curtain,
You cannot see Him outside His work.
Since His workshop is the abode of the wise one,
Whoso seeks Him without is ignorant of Him.
Come, then, into His workshop, which is Not-Being.
There you may see the Creator and creation at once.
Whoso has seen how bright is the workshop,
Sees how obscure is the outside of that shop.
Thou art hidden from us, though the heavens are filled
With Thy light, which is brighter than sun and moon!
Thou art hidden, yet revealest our hidden secrets!
Thou art the source that causes our rivers to flow.
Thou art like water, and we like the millstone.
Thou art like the wind and we like the dust;
The wind is unseen, but the dust is seen by all.
Thou art the spring, and we the sweet green garden;
Spring is not seen, though its gifts are seen.
Our every motion every moment testifies,
For it proves the presence of the Everlasting God.[21]


In the language of Sufi poets God is "the Beloved," and people the lover. They see the presence of God imminent in all beautiful things, but manifested most clearly and most fully in humanity.

"The real goal of Sufi," states E. W. Gibb, "is absorption in Deity. The highest happiness of any being consists in the most perfect realization of itself: the human soul realizes itself most perfectly in union with the Divine Soul, so therein lies its supreme felicity."

Omar, referring to this search for union with the Divine, declares:

---

[20] Rumi, translated by J. P. Brown.
[21] Rumi, translated by E. H. Whinfield.

The world is baffled in its search for Thee!
Wealth cannot find Thee, no, nor poverty:
All speak of Thee, but none have ears to hear,·
Thou art near to all, but none have eyes to see.[22]

The derivation of both Lover and Beloved is from Love,
which, in its abode of glory, is exempt from differentiation,
and, in the sanctuary of its own Identity, is sanctified from
inwardness and outwardness. Yea, in order to display its perfection, in such way as is identical with its essence and equally
identical with its attributes, it shows itself to itself in the
mirror of Lovehood and Belovedness, and reveals its Beauty
to its own contemplation by means of the Seer and the vision.

The Face is only one, yet multiple
When thou in many mirrors see'st it.[23]

The Sufis believe that the distance between God and man
could be eliminated by *Marifa*, or knowledge of God. According
to Mishkat Al Masabih, "he who approaches near to Me one
span, I will approach to him one cubit; and he who approaches
near to Me one cubit, I will approach near to him one fathom;
and whoever approaches Me walking, I will come to him running;
and he who meets Me with sins equivalent to the whole world, I
will greet him with forgiveness equal to it."

"The Sufis," states Edward G. Browne, "regard God as identical with pure being. . . . Sufism, then is an idealist pantheism.
To the Sufis everything speaks of God. He is everywhere and in
everything . . . and hidden only because so evident."

Baba Kubi of Shiraz refers to this doctrine:[24]

In the market, in the cloister—only God I saw
In the valley and in the mountain—only God I saw.
Him I have seen beside me oft in tribulation;
In favor and in fortune—only God I saw.

---

[22] Omar Khayyam, translated by E. H. Whinfield.
[23] Iraqi, translated by E. G. Browne.
[24] Baba Kubi of Shiraz, translated by R. A. Nicholson.

In prayer and fasting, in praise and contemplation,
In the religion of the prophet—only God I saw.
In prayer and fasting, in praise and contemplation,
In the religion of the prophet—only God I saw.
Neither soul nor body, accident nor substance,
Qualities nor causes—only God I saw.
I opened mine eyes and by the light of His Face
    around me
In all the eye discovered—only God I saw.
Like a candle I was melting in His fire:
Amidst the flames outflanking—only God I saw.
Myself with mine own eyes I saw most clearly,
But when I looked with God's eyes—only God I saw.
I passed away into nothingness, I vanished,
And lo, I was the All-living—only God I saw.

The Sufi's God is not at all like the God conceived by most
Christians, Jews, or Muslims. His creativity is not historical, not
accidental, not at all measurable. His work is continuous, with
no beginning and with no end. His work comes out of timelessness
and nothingness. God's bounty and blessing are sheer love, grac-
ing both friends and foes alike.

Nafasi, a Sufi mentor who lived in the latter part of the
thirteenth century, declares:

> The Sufis consider it an axiom that the world must have
> had a creator. They affirm that He is one, and omnipresent.
> He is one, ancient, First and Last, the End and Limit of all
> things, incomparable, unchangeable, indivisible, not subject to
> the laws of time, place or direction; the nature of God is an
> infinite and illimitable light a boundless and fathomless ocean,
> compared with which the entire universe is more insignificant
> than a drop of water in the sea. The love and proximity of
> God to all created being is the same, for the highest and lowest
> are alike in His sight.

The Sufi's experience is deeply and basically rooted in God
as Being, which is at once Being and not-Being. They see in
everything among God's creatures all the glories of His Being.

Jami, elaborating on this experience, contends that the essence of the Truth, most glorious and most exalted, is nothing

but Being. His Being is not subject to defect or diminution. He is untouched by change or variation and is exempt from plurality and multiplicity. He transcends all manifestations. Every "how" and "why" have made their appearance through Him; but in Himself He transcends every "how" and "why." Everything is perceived by Him, while He is beyond perception.

"Every beauty and perfection," continues Jami, "manifested in the theatre of the various grades of Being is a ray of His perfect beauty reflected therein. It is from these rays that exalted souls have received their impress of beauty and their quality of perfection."

> The Loved One's rose-parterre I went to see,
> That beauty's Torch espied me, and quoth He,
>   "I am the tree; the flowers my offshoot are.
>   Let not those offshoots hide from thee
>   the tree."[25]

Muhammad Ibn Wasi goes as far as to say that "I never saw anything without seeing the face of God in it."

Shible Numani (d. 1914) states: "I never saw anything except God."

"In mosques and tavern, in pagan and Muslim, only God I saw."

Usuli (d. 1532), enraptured, sees God in everything and in every place and nothing else:

> Each wave that riseth on the Sea of Absolute
>   Existency
> Declares that secret, "I am God" or openly or
>   secretly.
> All things are mine, and of their quintessential
>   nature they beget,
> Some gold, some silver, other stones and clouds
>   of earth, in verity.
> Although in truth this orchard hath one water
>   and one gardener,
> What myriad trees do grow herein from multiform
>   reality!

---

[25] Jami, translated by E. H. Whinfield.

Behold the race of men and see how some are poison,
   sugar some;
How great a marvel diverse fruits appearing on
   a single tree!
What myriad acts are ordered fair, what myriad
   shows are brought to naught;
How passing strange work is this, whereof
   no workmen we can see!
Lo, thou hast entered and shalt quit this
   nine-domed, hexagonal;
Yet neither entrance-door nor gate of exit of thee.

How sore must labor the adept 'ere he attain perfection's point.
What blood the mine must drain to form a single
   gem of radiancy.[26]

---

[26] Usuli, translated by E. G. W. Gibb.

# 9

## Shabastari, the Pillar and
## Interpreter of Sufism

My heart was hid from knowledge of itself by a hundred veils,
By pride and vanity and self-conceit and illusion.
That fair idol (The Truth) entered my door at early morn,
And wakened me from the sleep of negligence.
By his face the secret chamber of my soul was illumined.
He said to me, "O Pharisee and hypocrite,
To cast one glance at my face for half a moment,
Is worth a thousand years of devotion."

Shabastari.

In the writings of Sad Ud din Mahmud Shabastari, another
Sufi mentor, some ideas of the Sufi pantheism are clearly expressed. Shabastari's famous book *Gulshani Raz* was composed
in A.D. 1317. It is the answer to fifteen questions on the doctrines
of Sufism. Like a number of other Persian poets, little information as to the circumstances of his life and times is to be found in
his writings, or the writings of his contemporaries. We know
that he lived in Tabriz, and that he came in contact with a number of Christian missionaries who at the time resided in Tabriz
and were trying unsuccessfully to convert Mongol rulers of
Iran. In 1335, Mongol Emperor Ghazan Khan, with one hundred
thousand of his followers, adopted Islamic faith and expelled
the Christian missionaries. During the struggle between Muslim

176

and Christian missionaries for the salvation of the soul of the
Mongols, Tabriz was visited by the emissaries of Pope Nicholas
IV and Pope Boniface VIII, and also by Marco Polo. Shabastari's
acquaintance with Christian doctrines may have been derived
from his discussion with monks and missionaries who frequented
Tabriz at this time.

The first European authors to learn about *Gulshani Raz* were
the French travelers Chardin and Bernier, in A.D. 1700. Both of
them described *Gulshani Raz* as the "Summa Theologia" of the
Sufis.

1838, Von Hammer-Purgstall published a Persian text, with
a German verse translation. In 1880, E. H. Whinfield obtained
Hammer's copy and two Indian manuscripts and commentary and
translated them into English.

In his introduction to *Gulshani Raz*, Whinfield states:

> Many of the Catholic definitions of "mystical theology" would
> do for descriptions of Sufism. The ruling ideas in both sys-
> tems are very similar, if not absolutely identical. Thus, for
> instance, we find the Sufis talking of "love to God," of "Union
> with God," of "death to self," and "life eternal in God," of
> "the indwelling in man of the spirit," of "the nullity of works
> and ceremonies," of "grace and spiritual illumination," and
> of the "logos." Both systems may be characterized as religions
> of the heart, as opposed to formalism and ritualism. Both exalt
> the "inner heart" at the expense of the outward ordinance
> and voice of the Church. Both exhibit the same craving for
> visionary raptures and supernatural exaltations, and have been
> productive of similar excesses and extravagancies.[1]

Furthermore, Whinfield refers to the Sufi tendency to pantheism as expressed in *Gulshani Raz*, which has its counterpart
in that of Eckart and St. Bernard's Sermons on the Canticles,
the wonderful effusions of St. Theresa and the mystical hymns
of St. Alphonso Liquori and others.

Whinfield, after examining the source of the ideas of the
*Gulshani Raz*, admits that the pantheism of the Sufis as expounded

---

[1] Shabastari, *Gulshani Raz*, translated by E. H. Whinfield, (London: Trubner and
Co., 1880), p. 12.

by the Gulshan should not be confused with the modern European idea of pantheism. The latter, according to Bossuet, "makes everything God except God himself."

In the works of Shabastari we discover a different kind of pantheism. It is an amplification and expansion rather than minimization of the idea of the Divinity, infinite, omnipresent, and omnipotent. Shabastari believes in the sense of his own existence and his own freedom passing away and becoming absorbed in the sense of absolute dependence on this Infinite Being.

> By whose light the two worlds were illumined,
> By whose grace the dust of Adam bloomed with roses
> That Almighty One who in the twinkling of an eye,
> From *Kaf* and *Nun* [be created] brought forth
>    the two worlds.

> The world of command and that of creatures are
>    one, one becomes many and many few.

Compared with this omnipresent power, underlying all the universe, dominating man's will and heart, all other agencies in this world are nothing:

> He knows "the Truth", and to whom unity is
>    revealed,
> Sees at first glance the light of very Being
> Nay more, as he sees by illumination that pure light,
> He sees God first in everything that he sees.

> The whole universe is exposed to view by His light,
> But how is He exposed to view in the universe?
> The light of His essence is not contained in
>    phenomena,
> For the glory of His majesty is exceeding great.

> Know the world is a mirror from head to foot,
> In every atom are a hundred blazing suns.
> If you cleave the heart of one drop of water
> A hundred pure oceans emerge from it.
> If you examine closely each grain of dust,
> A thousand Adams may be seen in it.[2]

---

[2] Mahmud Shabastari, *Gulshani Raz*, translated by E. H. Whinfield, (London: Trubner and Co., 1880), pp. 14–15.

Shabastari's pantheism is only the corollary of the doctrine of Jabr (predestination) or compulsion to carry out the universal action of God. This is the same impulse that compels "men of a logical turn of mind to regard not only all the action but also all existence in the universe as the direct outcome or manifestation of the Divine energy."

According to Whinfield,

> The whole Sufi system follows as a logical consequence from this fundamental assumption. Sense and reason cannot transcend phenomena, or see the real Being which underlies them all; so sense and reason must be ignored and suspended in favor of the "inner light," the inspiration or divine illumination in the heart, which is the only faculty whereby men perceive the infinite. Thus the enlightened see that the whole external phenomenal world, including man's "self" is an illusion, non-existent in itself and, insofar as it is non-existent, evil— because it is a departure from the one real Being. Man's only duty is to shake off this illusion, this clog of Not-Being, to efface and die to self, and to be united with and live eternally in the one real Being—"the Truth."[3]

But to the majority of the Sufis the ultimate Reality is not only ultrasensuous but ultrarational. He is everywhere and yet nowhere. He is rational yet beyond reason. From Him all forms emerge, but He is formless. He is the nearest to us and yet so remote.

Sadi of the Shiraz states:

> The Friend [God] is nearer to me than myself,
> But it is more strange that I am far from Him:
> What am I to do? To whom can it be said that He
> Is in my arms, but I am exiled from Him.

He is at home only in the essence of the soul of man and the only realities are the divine and the human soul. The universe, whose identification with God leads to pantheism, sinks into nothingness. So we see that the logical and the cosmical

3 Ibid., pp. VII and VIII.

forms of pantheism can be identified with the mystic form of it only through confusion of ideas.[4]


God is the life of the universe and the universe is His body. The spirits and angels are the sources of this body and the heavens and the elements are its limbs. This is unity, and all else is fantasy.[5]

Shabastari believes that in our progress to union with God we have to abandon external observances, and outward forms profit little because they represent duality. God's divine light enters our heart when we expel self-righteousness, selfishness, and hatred. The manner in which this unity takes place is explained by Shabastari in his famous collection of poems, *Gulshani Raz*.

To the first question, what is that which they call thinking? Shabastari answers:

> Thinking is passing from the false to the truth,
> And seeing the Absolute Whole in the part.
> Philosophers who have written books on it,
> Say as follows when they are defining it.
> That when a conception is formed in the mind,
> It is first of all named reminiscence.
> And when you pass on from this in thinking,
> It is called by the learned interpretation.
> When conceptions are properly arranged in the mind,
> The result with logicians is known as thinking.
> From proper arrangement of known conceptions
> The unknown proposition becomes known.
> The major promise is a father, the minor a mother,
> And the conclusion a son, O brother!
> But to learn of what kind this arrangement is,
> Reference must be made to books of logic.
> Moreover, unless divine guidance aids it,
> Verily logic is mere bondage of forms.
> That road is long and hard, leave it,
> Like Moses for a season cast away that staff.

---

[4] Abdul Hakim Khalifa, *The Metaphysics of Rumi* (Lahore, Pakistan: Institute of Islamic Culture, 1965), pp. 153–54.
[5] Ibid., p. 152.

Come for a season into the "Valley of Peace,"
Hear with faith the call, "Verily I am God."
He that knows the "Truth", and to whom unity is
    revealed,
Sees at the first glance the light of very Being.
Nay more, as he sees by illumination that pure light,
He sees God first in everything that he sees;
Abstraction is a condition of good thinking,
For then the lightning of divine guidance illumines us.
To him, whom God guides not into the road,
It will not be disclosed by use of logic.
For as much as the philosopher is bewildered,
He sees in things nothing but the contingent,
From the contingent he seeks to prove the necessary.
Therefore is he bewildered at the essence of the
    necessary.
Sometimes he travels backward in a circle,
Sometimes he is imprisoned in the Chain of Proofs,
While his reason goes deep into phenomenal existence,
His feet are caught in the Chain of Proofs.
All things are manifested through their likes
But "The Truth" has neither rival nor peer,
I know not how you can know Him.
Necessary matter has no sample in contingent
How can man know it, tell me how?
Fool that he is! For he seeks the blazing sun
By the dim light of a torch in the desert.[6]

    In the above poem, Shabastari makes abstraction, or purification from self, a condition of good thinking. The Sufis explain abstraction as "passing by the stages of carnal lusts, and mental operations, and human pleasure and relations, and emerging from the limitation of self, which tells man's real essence."

    When Shabastari discusses man, first he refers to his universal character and his two great attributes, Universal Reason and Universal Soul. Universal Reason, the first emanation from the Absolute, is likened to Adam, and Universal Soul, the second attribute, to Eve. Man, according to Shabastari, was the first in the Divine thought, but the last in fact. "All things were created

---

[6] Shabastari, *Gulshani Raz*, pp. 7–9.

as subsidiary to man, and man is an end in himself, and not a means to any further end." He also refers to the Koran's statement, "And He said unto the angels, 'Worship Adam,' and they all worshipped him except Iblis [Satan]."[7]

The essence of man, therefore, is universal reason and soul, which animate all things and form the bond of mystical union between them and man.

In Shabastari's works, as well as in the works of most Sufi thinkers and writers, man's mind, intelligence, individuality, freedom, integrity, and universalism are most respected and revered. The Sufi thinkers who hated and abhorred the cruelty and callousness of their time used their poems and prose to admonish kings and clergy for their shortcomings and to invite them to respond to the needs of their fellowmen. These Sufi poets and thinkers were whole men, universal men, compassionate men, sensitive to the sufferings and misery of their communities, and friends of helpless and needy people. They had a hatred of tyranny and a contempt for pomp, power, and wealth. They expressed this feeling as often and as strongly as they could. They strived to eliminate slavery and exploitation of man. They preached the Gospel of the dignity and freedom of mankind, opposed falsehood, wrongdoing, hatred, and greed. They asked man to ponder about his origin, his mission, and his purpose in life. They had firm conviction that their aim was to seek for the truth and serve the truth, regardless of consequences.

One finds in Shabastari and other Sufi poets a rare synthesis, an awareness of life's tragedy and complexity, of man's virtues and vices, and of his hopes and dreams.

> Ponder well once for all on your own origin,
> Your first mother had a father who was also her
>     mother.
> Behold the world entirely comprised in yourself,
> That which was made last was first in thought.
> The last that was made was the soul of Adam,
> The two worlds were a means to his production.
> There is no other final cause beyond man,
> It is disclosed in man's own self.

---

[7] Koran 2:32.

You are the reflection of "the Adored of Angels."
For this cause are you worshipped of angels.
Each creature that goes before you has a soul,
And from that soul is bound a cord to you.
You are the kernel of the world in the midst thereof.
Know yourself that you are the world's soul.
The world of reason and mind is your stock in trade,
Earth and heavens are your vesture.
Behold this Not Being which is the evidence of
    Being,
See this height now it is the essence of depth.
Hence you learn all the names of God,
For that you are an image reflected from the Named.
Power and Knowledge and Will are shown forth
If you, O slave of the Lord of Bliss!
You are the Hearing, Seeing, Living, Speaking,
Yet you endure not of yourself but of Him!
O first who are also the essence of the last!
O inner who are also the essence of the outward.
You day and night are cogitating about yourself,
It is most meet that you should think on self no more.

The phenomenal world, according to Shabastari, is in itself Not Being, wherein are reflected, as in a mirror, the various attributes of Being. Each part of their universe, therefore, is a reflection of the divine attribute. To reach this stage of divine attribute and to see God in everything, one has to set on the "journey up to God" and the "journey down from God in God," in a sort of circuit, and he who completes the circuit is faced with His Creator.

Man reaches this stage when he realizes that all things are one and represent God. Then he dies to self and lives with a regenerate heart in God. He sweeps away anything that hides God from him and "breaks through to the oneness." Service and good works raise men to a laudable station, but so long as division, greed, anger, and selfishness rule the hearts of people, a true mystical union of knower and known is not attained.

The man attains to the secret of unity
Who is not detained at the stages on the road.
But the knower is he that sees Very Being;

He that witnesses Absolute Being
He recognizes no Being but Very Being,
Being such as his own he gambles clean away.
Your Being is naught but thorns and weeds,
Cast it all clean away from you.
Go sweep out the chamber of your heart,
Make it ready to be the dwelling-place of the
   Beloved.
When you depart out, He will enter in.
In you, void of yourself, will He display His beauty.
The man who is loved for his "pious works,"
Whom the pains of "negation" purify as a room that
   is swept,
He finds an abode in a "laudable station,"
He finds a portion in "what eye hath not seen,
   nor ear heard."
But while the stain of his own being remains on him,
The knowledge of the Knower assumes not the form
   of experience.
Until you cast away obstacles from before you,
The light enters not the chamber of your heart.
As there are four obstacles in this world,
So also the modes of purification from them are four:
First, purification from filthiness of the flesh;
Second, from sin and evil, "whisper of the tempter,"
The third is the purification from bad habits,
Which make men as beasts of the field.
The fourth is the purification of secret,
For at this point the pilgrim's journeyings cease.
Whoso is cleaned with these purifications
Verily he is fit to see and commune with God.[8]

Sadi declares:

> I desired my Beloved, but when I saw Him
> I was dumbfounded and possessed neither
>    tongue nor eye.

On the other hand, Mansur Hallaj declares, "Verily, I am the Truth." Shabastari comments on this claim:

---

[8] Shabastari, *Gulshani Raz*, p. 41.

Verily, "I am the Truth" is a revelation of
  absolute mystery.
Save the Truth, who can say "I am the Truth"?
All the atoms of the world, like Mansur,
You will take to be drunken and heavy with wine.
Continually are they singing this song of praise,
Continually dwelling on this mystic verity.
When you have carded "self" as cotton
You, like Mansur Hallat will raise the cry
Take out the cotton of your illusion from your ears,
Hearken to the call of the One, the Almighty.
This call is ever coming to you from "the Truth,"
Why are you tarrying for the last day?
Come into "the valley of the Peace" for straightway
The bush will say to you "verily I am God."
The saying "I am the Truth" was lawful for the bush,
Why is it unlawful in the mouth of a good man?
Every man whose heart is pure from doubt,
Knows for sure that there is no Being but "one,"
Saying, "I am" belongs only to "The Truth,"
For essence is absent, and illusive appearance
  is absent.
"I," "We," "Thou," and "He," are all one thing,
For in unity there is distinction of persons.
Every man who as a void is empty of self,
Re-echoes within him the cry, "I am the Truth;"
He takes his eternal side, other perishes,
Travelling, travel, and traveller all become one.
Incarnation and communion spring from "other,"
But very Unity comes from the mystic journey.


Shabastari's mystical idealism supplies the reader with a powerful antidote against the pessimistic tendencies evoked by the daily tensions and mental agonies in the age of trouble and uncertainty. He, like other Sufi writers, helps us to see the goodness and nobility of human nature, the immortality, greatness, and virtue of the spirit of man. No wonder that the noble ideas and the pantheistic idealism of these great men have been treasured by millions of people all over the world. It is such a joy to listen to Hafiz when he declares:

They are calling to me from the pinnacles
of the Throne of God:
I know not what hath kept me in this
dust-heap [the world].

Shabastari believes that man is the soul of the world—the microcosm. While other creatures reflect only single divine attributes, man reflects them all. He is an epitome of the universe, and so by introspection he may see in himself reflection of all the divine attributes—of the fullness of the Godhead.

He is the perfect man who in all perfection
Does the work of a slave in spite of his lordliness.
Afterwards, when he has finished his course,
"The Truth" sets on his head the Crown of Khalifate.
He finds eternal life after dying to self, and again
He runs another course from his end to his beginning.
He makes the law his upper garment,
He makes the mystic path his inner garment.
But know very truth is the station of his nature,
He comprehends both infidelity and faith
Being imbued with fair virtues,
And famed for knowledge, devotion and piety,
All these in him, but he far from all these,
Overshadowed beneath the canopy of Divine Epiphanies.[9]

To be a haunter of taverns is to be freed from
    self,
Self-regard is paganism, even if it be in
    righteousness.
They have brought you news from the tavern
That unification is shaking off relations.
The tavern is of the world that has no similitude,
It is the place of lovers that reck not.
The tavern is the nest of the bird of the soul,
The tavern is the sanctuary that has no place
The tavern-haunter is desolate in a desolate place,
In his desert the world is as a mirage.

---

[9] According to the Koran: We are about to place man on earth as Khalif (the Vice-Regent of God).

Shabastari concludes his discussion by explaining the Sufi conception of God and the universe, and their ecstatic experiences. This conception may seem strange and irreverent to many believers, but it seems respectful and appropriate to the Sufis. As Xenophanes stated, our conception of God has a constant relation to our own state of mind and moral and intellectual stature. Symbols that we see to be inadequate and misleading, ideas that we consider utopian and beyond the reach of human action, were adored and appreciated by the Sufis:

Whatsoever is seen in this visible world
Is as a reflection from the sun of that world.
The world is as curl, down, mole and brew,
For everything in its own place is beautiful.
The epiphany is now in beauty, now in majesty,
Cheek and curl are the similitudes of those
    verities.
The attributes of "The Truth" are mercy and
    vengeance,
Cheek and curl of fair ones are types of these two.
When these words are heard by the sensual ear,
At first they denote objects of sense.
The spiritual world is infinite,
How can finite words attain to it?
He finds a portion in what eye hath not seen,
    nor ear heard!
But while the stain of his own being remains on him,
The knowledge of the knower assumes not the form
    of experience.
Until you cast away obstacles from before you,
The light enters not the chamber of your heart.
As there are four obstacles in this world,
So also the modes of purification from them are four.
First, purification from filthiness of the flesh;
Second, from sin and evil "whispers of the tempter";
The third is the purification from bad habits,
Which make men as beasts of the field;
The fourth is the purification of the secrets,
For at this point the pilgrim's journey ceases.
Whoso is cleaned with these purifications,
Verily he is fit to commune with God.

The principles of a good character are equity,
And thereafter wisdom, temperance, courage.
He who is endowed with all these four
Is a sage perfect in thought and deed.
His soul and heart are well informed with wisdom,
He is neither over cunning nor a fool.
By temperance his appetites are subdued,
Intemperance and insensibility alike are banished.
The courageous man is pure from objectiveness and
     from boasting,
His nature is exempt from cowardice and rashness.
Equity is as the garment of his nature,
He is void of injustice, thus his character is good.
All the virtues lie in the mean,
Which is alike removed from excess and defect.
The mean is as the "narrow way,"
On either side yawns hell's bottomless pit.
In fineness and sharpness as a sword
One may not turn round nor stand on it long.
Since equity has only one opposite vice,
The total number of opposite vices is seven.
Beneath each number is hidden a mystery,
For this cause has hell seven gates.
Like as hell is prepared for iniquity.
Light and mercy are the recompense of equity,
Darkness and cursing the requital of iniquity.
Goodness is made manifest in equity,
Equipoise in body is its summit of perfection.
Since a compound is as one entity,
It is remote from its parts in its nature and
     differentia.
It becomes like to a simple essence,
And between it and simple essence there is a bond;
Not that bond which subsists between the compound
     and its parts,
(For spirit is free from the attributes of
     corporality,
But when water and clay are purified altogether,
Spirit is added to them by "The Truth."

Shabastari, like other Sufi poets, discusses many ideas and
uses many expressions borrowed from Zoroaster's writings. He

states that the illusion of free will is Magianism, setting up an
evil first cause, *Ahriman,* over against the good God, *Yazdan.*
This illusion, according to Shabastari must be shaken off and
annihilated in the conviction that the only free agent is "The
Truth," and man is a passive instrument in His hands, and absolutely dependent on His pleasure. Man's glory, continues Shabastari, lies in abandoning his self-will, and in finding his true
will in God's will:

> While you are cloaked in this self of yours,
> The world is always as a veil before your eyes.
> Then you are the lowest part of the circle of
>      being,
> Then you are most opposed to the point of unity;
> The phenomena of the world overpower you,
> Thence like Satan you say, "who is like unto me"?
> Then you say, "I myself have free-will,"
> My body is the horse and my soul the rider,
> "The reins of the body are in the hand of the soul,"
> The entire direction thereof is given to me.
> Know you not that all this is the road of the
>      Magicians,
> All there lies and deception come from illusive
>      existence?
> How, O foolish man, can free-will appertain
> To a person whose essence is nothingness?
> Seeing that your being is all one with not being,
> Say whence comes this free-will of yours?
> A man whose real existence is not of himself,
> Is neither good nor evil in his own essence.
> Whom have you seen in the whole world
> Who ever once acquired pleasure without pain?
> Who continued ever at his pitch of perfection?
> Dignities are permanent, but men of dignity
> Are subject to the sway of "The Truth." Allah
>      is over all.
> Recognize the "working" of "The Truth" in every
>      place,
> Place not foot beyond your own proper limits.
> Ask of your own state that this free-will is,
> And thence know who are men of free-will.

Every man whose faith is other than predestination,
Is according to the prophet even as a Zoroastrian
Like as those Zoroastrians speak of Yazdan and
    Ahriman,
So these ignorant fools say "I" and "He."
The attribution of actions to us is imaginary,
That attribution itself is but a play and a farce.
You existed not when your actions were originated,
You were appointed to fulfill a certain purpose.
By the uncaused sovereign will of "The Truth,"
By His fore-knowledge giving absolute command,
There was predestined, before soul and body were,
For every man his appointed work;
Man has no free-will, but is under compulsion;
Ah, poor creature, seeming to be free, yet a slave!
This is not justice, but true fore-knowledge and
    justice;
This is not oppression, but pure mercy and grace.
He has imposed on you the law for this cause,
That He has imparted to you of His essence.
Since you are impotent in the hands of "The Truth,"
Abandon and forsake this self of yours.
In "The All" you will obtain deliverance from self,
In "The Truth" you will become rich, O Dervish!
Go, Soul of your father! Yield yourself to God's
    will,
Resign yourself to the Divine fore-ordinance.

Shabastari condemns arrogance and selfishness. He also has
no respect for those who show disrespect for the ideas and religions and faiths different from those of their own:

How can the mysteries beheld in ecstatic vision
Be interpreted by spoken words?
When mysteries treat of these mysteries,
They interpret them by types.
For objects of sense are as shadows of that world,
And this world is as an infant, and that as the nurse,
I believe that these words were at first assigned
To those mysteries in their original usage.
The license of mystics is in three "states,"
Annihilation, intoxication and the fever of love.

All who experience these three "states"
Know the use of these words and their meanings.
But if you experience not these "states"
Be not an ignorant infidel blindly repeating them.
These mystic "states" are not mere illusions,
All men reach not the mysteries of the mystic path.
Oh friend, vain babbling proceeds not from men of
    truth,
To know these states requires either revelation or faith.
I have explained the usage of words and their meanings
To you in brief, and if you attend you will understand.
In applying them look to their final intent,
And regard all the attributes of each.
Use them in comparisons in manner proper thereto,
Carefully abstain from applying them otherwise.


Wine, torch and beauty all are present,
Neglect not to embrace that beauty.
Quaff the wine of dying to self, and for a season
Peradventure you will be freed from the dominion of
    self.
Drink wine that it may set you free from yourself,
And may conduct the being of the drop to the ocean.
Drink wine, for its cup is the face of "The Friend,"
The cup is His eye drunken and flown with wine.
Seek wine without cup or goblet,
Wine is wine-drinker, cupbearer is winecup.
Drink wine from the cup of "the face that endures,"
The text "their Lord gave them to drink" is its cup-
    bearer.
Pure wine is that which gives you purification.
Drink wine and rid yourself of coldness of heart,
For a drunkard is better than the self-righteous.
When a ray from His face falls upon the wine,
Many forms are seen on it as it were bubbles.
World and spirit world are seen on it as bubbles.
Its bubbles are to the saints as veils.
Universal reason is dazed and beside itself at this,
Universal soul is reduced to slavery.
The whole universe is as His winehouse,
The heart of every atom is His winecup.
Reason is drunken, angels drunken, soul drunken,

Air drunken, earth drunken, heaven drunken.
The heavens giddy with this wine are reeling to and fro,
Desiring in their heart to smell its perfume.
The angels drinking it pure from pure vessels,
Pour the dregs of their draught upon this world.
The elements becoming light-headed from that draught
Fall now into the fire, now into the water.
From the scent of its dregs which fell on the earth,
Man ascends up 'til he reaches heaven.

One from the scent of its dregs becomes a philosopher,
One from seeing the colour of the pure wine a
   traditionalist,
One from half a draught becomes righteous,
One from quaffing a cupful becomes a lover.
Yet another swallows at one draught
Cup, winehouse, cup bearer and wine drinker.
He swallows them all, yet his mouth remains open.

While in this last quarter of the twentieth century, people
still hate, feud, and fight on account of nationality, color, creed,
and ideology, Shabastari six hundred years ago expressed not
only tolerance, but respect and reverence for all the religions:

Here idol is the evidence of love and unity,
Girdle is the binding of the bond of obedience
Since infidelity and faith are both based on Being,
Idol-worship is essentially unification.
Since all things are the manifestation of Being,
One amongst them must be an idol.
Consider well, O wise man,
An idol as regards its real being is not vain.
Know that God most High created it,
And whatever comes from the good is good.
Being is purely good in whatever it be,
If it also contains evil, that proceeds from "other",
If the Muslim but knew what is faith,
He would see that faith is idol-worship.
If the polytheist only knew what idols are,
How would he be wrong in his religion?
He sees in idols naught but the visible creature,
And that is the reason that he is legally a heathen.

You also, if you see not "The Truth" hid in the idols,
In the eye of the law are not a Muslim.
By telling beads and saying prayers and reading the Quoran
The man becomes not a musulman.
That man is disgusted with superficial faith,
To whom the true infidelity has once been revealed.
Within every body is hidden a soul,
And within infidelity is hidden true faith.
Infidelity is ever giving praise to "The Truth",
The text, "All things praise God", proves it. Who can
    gainsay it?
What am I saying? I have gone astray from the road?
"Learn then, and after all that is revealed, say, God"
Who adorned the face of the idol with such beauty?
Who became an idol-worshipper, unless "The Truth willed it?"
It is He that made, He that said, He that is,
Made good, said good, is good.
See but one, say one, know but one,
In this are summed up the roots and branches of faith.
It is not I who declare this, hear it from the Quoran.
"There is no distinction in the creatures of the merciful."

Shabastari warns his readers against being drowned in the ocean of fantasy and illusion: "Rest not in the illusion of sense and reason, but abandon your 'natural realism' as Abraham abandoned the worship of the host of heaven. Press on, 'til like Moses at Mount Sinai, you see the Mount of your illusive phenomenal existence annihilated at the approach of Divine Glory. Ascend like Christ and Muhammad to heaven, and behold the mighty sings of Lord."

Thus illumined we will see "The Truth" to be the source of all being, diffused and poured out into the phenomenal world by means of the various emanations, beginning with the Logos and ending with man.

Shabastari's contact with Christian missionaries in Tabriz, and his Sufi belief that all religions represent different approaches to "The Truth," enables him to devote a large part of his book to Christianity:

In Christianity, the end I see is purification from self,
Deliverance from the yoke of bondage.

The blessed portal of Unity is the sanctuary of the Soul,
Which is the nest of the everlasting-phoenix
This doctrine was taught by God's spirit [Jesus],
Who proceeded from the Blessed Spirit.
Also by God is placed in you a Soul,
Wherein is a sample of the Blessed Spirit.
If you find release from the carnal mind of humanity
You will obtain entrance to the life of Divinity.
Every man who is purified as angels are pure
Will ascend with God's Spirit to the fourth heaven.[10]

From gold and women comes naught but store of pain,
Abandon them as Jesus abandoned Mary.
Be a true believer and forsaking the bond of sects,
Enter the cloister of faith as Christian monk.
While "other" and "others" are set before your eyes,
Though you be in a mosque, it is no better than a
    Christian cloister.
When the vesture of "other" passes out of sight,
The cloister becomes to you as a mosque.
I know not in what religious state you are,
Cast out your adversary the flesh, that you may escape.
Idols, girdles, Christianity and church bells
All indicate the renouncing of name and fame.
If you would become a faithful servant,
Prepare yourself in faithfulness and sincerity.
Go, take yourself out of your own road,
Every moment renew your faith.

When I had drained that pure draught to the last drop
I fell beside myself on the bare dust.
Now I neither exist in myself, nor do I not exist,
I am not sober, not sick, not drunken.
Sometimes like His eye I am joyful,
Sometimes like His curls I am fluttering.
Sometimes by force of nature I am lying on ashes,
Sometimes at a look from Him I am in the *rose garden*.

While infidelity dwells in your inmost Soul,
Be not satisfied with this outward Islam

---

10 Shabastari, *Gulshani Raz.*

Of yourself every moment renew your faith,
Be a believer, Be a believer, Be a believer![11]
Verily faith is born of infidelity,
That is not infidelity from which faith is increased.
Abandon study to be seen and heard of men,
Cast off the Dervish cloak, bind on Magian girdle.
Be as our Magian sage in pure infidelity,
If you are a man, give your heart to manliness.
Purge yourself from affirmation and negations,
Give your mind wholly to the young Christians.

Idols and young Christians are the Light made manifest,
For it finds its exponent in the idol's face.
It leads captive all hearts,
It is now the minstrel,—now the cupbearer.

What a minstrel is he who by one sweet melody[12]
Burns up the garners of a hundred devotees!
What a cupbearer is he who by a single cup
Makes drunken two hundred men of threescore and ten!
If he enters the mosque at early dawn,
He leaves not a single wakeful man therein.
If he enters the cloister drunken at night,
He makes Sufis' stories an empty tale.
He makes one faithful, another an infidel,
He fills the world with tumult and wrong.
Taverns have been edified by his lips,
Mosques have been illumined by his cheek.
All my desire has been accomplished through him,
Through him I gained deliverance from infidel lust.
My heart was hid from knowledge of itself by a
    hundred veils.

By pride and vanity and self-conceit and illusion.
That fair idol entered my door at early morn,
And wakened me from the sleep of negligence.
By his face the secret chamber of my soul was illumined.
Thereby I saw what I myself really am.

---

[11] Koran, Sura 11, 59: "verily Muslims and Jews and Christians and Sabeites—
whoever of these believeth in God and the last day, and doetth that which is
right, shall have his reward with the Lord."
[12] It is the effect of preaching the truth.

When I cast a look on his fair face
I heaved a sigh of wonder from my soul.
He said to me, "O Pharisee and hypocrite,
Thy life has been spent in seeking name and fame
Behold this knowledge, devotion, self-seeking and
    illusion.
From what have they kept thee back, O laggard!
To cast one glance on my face for half a moment,
Is worth a thousand years of devotion."

In summary the face of that world-adorner
Was disclosed and unveiled before my eyes.
The face of my soul was blackened with shame
To think of my life lost and my wasted days.
But when that moon, whose face was as the sun,
Saw that I had cast away hope from my soul,
He filled a goblet and gave me to drink,
And from that draught fire was kindled within me.
"Now", quoth he, "with this wine, tasteless and odourless,
Wash from thee the writing on the tablet of Being."

# Epilogue

In the course of this study we have tried to show how Sufis combined ancient Iran's legacy of respect for human dignity and rights with Christian love, Islamic tradition of universalism and egalitarianism, Hindu practice of piety and annihilation, and Judaic belief in one God. To this combination was added the mystical idea of the unification of man with God. Throughout centuries Sufi poets and thinkers fulfilled a variety of functions for their communities: social, charitable, intellectual, psychological, and sometimes political, as well as those which we might consider spiritual and mystical. They were considered as conscience of their society and as missionaries in the cause of love, justice, harmony, and brotherhood.

In many instances these poets and intellectuals have achieved a popular and even spiritual and political influence never matched by any other leader. There are no peers for Rumi, Hafiz, Sanai, Attar, Al-Ghazali, Shabastari, and scores of other Sufi poets and pundits in Iran or in any other Muslim community. The traditional religious and political forces in the Islamic world throughout different areas underwent a gradual change and reform under the onslaught of Sufi poets' ideas.

Their amazing impact on the society could be judged by the vicious criticism and attacks of orthodox religious groups.

In these attacks, a number of elements may be discerned. Politically they were accused of being disloyal to the country and the king for not accepting the official religion of the state and the oppressive rules and laws; socially they were considered to be "too close to folk Islam and too far from the Sharia" (the law of Islam). It was also suggested that Sufis showed cultural hostility and generated undesirable innovations and unpopular ideas. They were also assaulted for their lack of respect for religious rituals, their way of life, clothing, and long hair. In other words, the Sufi style was as much a shock to the orthodox and conservative Muslims as hippies are to the John Birch Society.

It was this hostility that caused the crucifixion of Hallaj, excommunication of Hafiz, imprisonment of Attar, and oppression of many other Sufi saints and savants.

The trouble with the orthodox leaders was that they could not understand that Sufism was an antithesis to their tyrannical way of life.

In Sufism there was very little room left for doctrinal and authoritative theological thought. The heart of Sufism as presented by Rumi, Sanai, Hafiz, Shabastari, Shible, and others was the loving, venerating attitude toward man and interpretation of religion as mystical experience for spreading love, brotherhood, harmony, and service. They were the sworn enemy of hatred, hypocrisy, prejudice, religious conflict, and greed.

More than once the Sufis attacked religious fanaticism, exclusiveness, backwardness, and narrow-mindedness.

It seems apparent from the works of Rumi, Hafiz, Attar, and other Sufi poets that the best tradition of Sufism is far removed from theology, fanaticism, church hierarchy, institutional stagnation, and compulsory conversion.

The mysticism of love and suffering, which teaches man to strive for unity with his creator, is perhaps the most important message of Sufism.

Rumi eloquently describes this aspect of the Sufi message:

In this tale there is a warning for thee, O soul,
That thou mayest acquiesce in God's ordinances,
And be wary and not doubt God's benevolence,
When sudden misfortunes befall thee.
Let others grow pale from fear of ill fortune,
Do thou smile like the rose at loss and gain;
For the rose, though its petals be torn asunder,
Still smiles on, and it is never cast down.

It says, "Why should I fall into grief in disgrace?"
I gather beauty even from the thorn of disgrace.
Whatsoever is lost to thee through God's decree
Know of a surety is so much gained from misfortune.
What is Sufism? Tis to find joy in the heart
Whensoever distress and care assail it.
Know troubles to be that eagle of the prophet's
Which carried off the sandal of that holy one,
In order to save his foot from the bite of the viper—
O Excellent device!—to preserve him from harm.
'Tis said, "Mourn not for your slaughtered cattle
If a wolf has hurried your flocks;"
For that calamity may avert a greater calamity,
And that loss may ward off a more grievous loss.

In the adorations and benedictions of righteous men
The praises of all the prophets are kneaded together.
All their praises are mingled into one stream,
All the vessels are emptied into one ocean.
Because He that is praised is, in fact only one,
In this respect all religions are only one religion.
Because all praises are directed towards God's light,
Their various forms and figures are borrowed from it.
Men never address praises but to one deemed worthy,
They err only through mistaken opinions of Him.
So when a light falls upon a wall,
That wall is a connecting-link between all its beams;
Yet when it casts that reflection back to its source,
It wrongly shows great as small, and halts in its praises
Or if the moon be reflected in a well,
And one looks down the well, and mistakenly praises it,
In reality he is intending to praise the moon,
Although, through ignorance, he is looking down the well.
The object of his praises is the moon, not its reflection;
His identity arises from mistake of the circumstances.

With the fine sensitivity and acute susceptibility that ir-
radiate the Sufi's poetry, it is remarkable how these liberal-
hearted poets preserved the strength and the majesty of their
minds in the face of opposition, oppression, and cruel treatment.
Hafiz, referring to these brutal and nerve-shattering events, states:

What is this anarchy that I see in this insane world? I see all
this planet full of conflict and chaos.

So deeply committed were Sufis in mystic unity, love, and universalism, that in every statement, ode, and lyric they expressed
their lofty themes. In Sufism there is no room for hatred, conflict, and religious strife.[1]

> Ignore the conflicts of all the seventy-two sects;
> since they could not find the facts they settled
> for fantasy.

> The fire of deceit and hypocrisy will consume the
> harvest of piety and religion;
> Hafiz, cast off this woolen cloak and be gone.

> My heart is weary of hypocrisy and this deceit,
> O happy the day, when I retire to the wine-tavern!

To Hafiz love is a mighty ocean full of dangers and terror;
but life without it is worse than death. Only through love we
live again:

> Muslims all! I love that idol
> With a true and jealous zeal;
> Not for dalliance, but bewildered
> In amazement here I kneel.
> What is love? A mighty ocean,
>     and of flame its waters are,
> Waters that are very mountains,
>     black as night, and swarming far.

> Dangerous, fierce and full of terror
> Crouch upon its waveswept rim,
> While a myriad sharks of judgment
> In its swelling billows swim.

> I was dead; the waters drowned me;
> Lo, the marvel, now I live

---

[1] Riza-Zadeh Shafaq, Tarikh Adabiyat-i Iran (Teheran: Ministry of Education,
1942), pp. 330–36.

And have found a gem more precious
Than the treasured worlds can give.

Rumi in his definition of Sufi and Saint, concludes:

What makes the Sufi? Purity of heart!
Not the patched mantle and the lust perverse
   of those vile earth-bound men who steal his name.
He in dregs discerns the essence pure:
In hardship ease, in tribulation joy.
The phantom sentries, who with baton drawn
Guard beauty's palace-gate and curtained bower
Give way before him, unafraid he passes,
And showing the king's arrow, enters in.

There is water that flows down from Heaven
To cleanse the world of sin by grace divine.
At last, its whole stock spent, its virtue gone,
Dark with pollution not its own, it speeds
Back to the fountain of all purities;
Whence, freshly bathed, earthward it sweeps again,
Trailing a robe of glory bright and pure.

This water is the spirit of the saints,
Which ever sheds, until itself is beggared,
God's balm on the sick soul; and then returns
To Him who made the purest light of Heaven.[2]

Ye who would search into the truth beware
Of false instructors, who assume the name
Of Sufi, and the woolen garment wear
Only to hide their inward sin and shame,
Like false Museilima [the false prophet] who
   dared to claim
The honors due to Muhammad's self alone,
Till in God's time the retribution came.
Good wine and bad are by their perfume known,
And only in results are truth and falsehood shown.[3]

---

[2] Rumi, Masnavi, translated by R. A. Nicholson.
[3] Rumi, Masnavi, translated by E. H. Palmer.

The unbeliever and the believer, according to Rumi, both proclaim the praise of God. Since believer and unbeliever practice accordingly, and that which God most high has promised comes to pass precisely, neither more nor less, it follows, then, that both proclaim the praises of God, the one with one tongue and the other with another.

Attar, in an eloquent statement, expresses the "state" of a Sufi's feelings and emotions:

> We are the Magians of old,
> Islam is not the faith we hold;
> In irreligion is our fame,
> And we have made our creed a shame.
>
> Now to the tavern we repair
> To gamble all our substance there,
> Now in the monastery cell
> We worship with the infidel.
>
> When Satan chances us to see
> He doffs his cap respectfully,
> For we have lessons to impart
> To Satan in the tempter's art.
>
> We were not in such nature made
> Of any man to be afraid;
> Head and foot in naked pride
> Like Sultans o'er the earth we ride.
>
> But we, alas, aweary are
> And the road is very far;
> We know not by what way to come
> Unto the place that is our home.
>
> And therefore we are in despair
> How to order our affair
> Because, wherever we have sought,
> Our minds were utterly distraught.
>
> When shall it come to pass, and when,
> That suddenly, beyond our ken,

We shall succeed to rend this veil
That doth our whole affair conceal?

What veil soever after this
Apparent to our vision is,
With the flame of knowledge true
We shall consume it through and through.

Where at the first in that far place
We came into the world of space,
Our soul by travail in the end
To that perfection shall ascend.

And so shall Attar shattered be
And rapt in sudden ecstasy
Soar to godly vision, even
Beyond the veils of earth and heaven.[4]

Hafiz, also in the following verses, summarizes the essence
of the Sufi faith:

Within the Magian tavern
    the light of God I see;
In such a place, O wonder!
    Shines out such radiancy.

Boast not, O leader of pilgrims,
    The privilege of thee.
Thou viewest God's own Temple;
    God shows Himself to me.

The house of hope is built on sand,
And life's foundations rest on air;
Then come, give wine unto my band
That we may make an end of care.

Let me be slave to that man's will
Who 'neath high heaven's turquoise bowl
Hath won and winneth freedom still
From all entanglements of soul.

---

[4] A. J. Arberry, *Persian Poems* (London: Everyman's Library, 1964), pp. 44–45.

Last night as toping I had been
In tavern, shall I tell to thee
What message from the world unseen
A heavenly angel brought to me?

Falcon of sovereign renown,
High-nesting bird of lofty gaze
This corner of affliction town
Befits thee ill, to pass thy days.

Hearest thou not the whistle's call
From heaven's rampart shrills for thee?
What chanced I cannot guess at all
This snare should now thy prison be.

Heed now the counsel I give,
And be it to thy acts applied;
For these are words I did receive
From Him that was my ancient guide.

Be pleased with what the fates bestow,
Nor let thy brow be furrowed thus;
The gate to freedom here below
Stands not ajar to such as us.

Look not to find fidelity
Within a world so weakly stayed;
This ancient crone, ere flouting thee,
A thousand bridegrooms had betrayed.

Take not for sign of true intent
Not think the rose's smile sincere;
Sweet, loving nightingale, lament.
There is much cause for weeping here.

What envying of Hafiz's ease?
Poor poetaster, dost thou mean
To make sweet music, and to please.
That is a gift of God alone.

Rumi in a special prayer beseeches God to free man from instability, envy, deceit, hypocrisy, and brutality!

O Thou that givest aliment and power and stability,
Set free the people from their instability.
To the soul that is bent double by envy
Give uprightness in the path of duty,
Give them self-control, "weigh down their scales,"
Release them from the arts of deceivers.
Redeem them from envying, O gracious one,
That through envy they be not stoned like Iblis (Satan)[5]
Even in their fleeting prosperity, see how the people
Burn up wealth and men through envy!
Read the story of "Wais and Ramin" and "Khosrow and Shirin,"[6]
To see what these fools have done to one another.
Lovers and beloved have both perished;
And not themselves only, but their love as well.
In the heart that is no heart envy comes to a head
That being trouble nonentity.[7]

Sadi, discussing the weakness of man because of ambition, greed, pride, and envy, states:

The proud man sees no one but himself
Because he has the veil of conceit in front;
If he were endowed with a God discerning eye,
He would see that no one is weaker than himself.

An ill-humored man insulted a Sufi who patiently bore it, saying: "O hopeful young man! I am worse than thou speakest of me, for I am more conscious of my faults than thou."

An ambitious minister of the king paid a visit to the great Sufi teacher Dhulnoun and asked for his favor, saying: "I am day and night engaged in the service of the Sultan hoping for his rewards, but at the same time I live in the state of fear and anxiety."

Dhulnoun wept and said, "Had I feared God the Great and Glorious, as thou fearest the Sultan, I should be amongst the righteous."

[5] According to the Koran, Satan was banished because of his envy of Adam.
[6] Wais and Ramin and Khosrow and Shirin are two Persian love stories that ended in tragedy because of envy.
[7] Rumi, Masnavi, translated by E. H. Whinfield.

If there were no hope of reward and fear of trouble,
The "state" of the Sufi would be as high as heaven
If the minister feared God as much
As he dreaded the Sultan he would be ranked with
    the Angels.


Ten Sufis may sleep under the same blanket, but one continent cannot hold two Shahs. When a pious Sufi eats half a loaf of bread, he bestows the other upon Dervishes. If a padishah were to conquer the seven continents, he would still in the same way covet another one.


I heard that men of God have not distressed the hearts of enemies. How canst thou attain that dignity who quarrellest and wagest war against friends?


The outward states of Sufi is the patched dress;
It suffices as a display to the face of the people.
The abandoning of the ego, of lust, and of desire
Is sanctity; not the abandonment of the robe only.[8]

The Persian Sufi literature is so vast, so rich and enormous, that it will take many volumes even to summarize it. However, it would be safe to assume that many of the contents of these books have considerable application in ethical terms for men and women in the world today:

Though you serve and help others, you shall look for
    no reward.

Any blessings, merits and advantages you may acquire
    transfer it to others without expecting any
    compensation.

God created all the people as his children and you
    shall look upon people of different colors, creed

---

[8] Sadi, Gulistan (Rose Garden), translated by Sir Richard Burton (London: Philip Allan & Co., 1928), pp. 24–63.

and race as equals without discrimination or distinction. Allow no impediments to arise in your mind
regarding your fellow men.

The ways to God are as many as the number of the people
of the world.

Reflect upon your errors, and shall not speak of
the faults of others.

In whatever venture you are engaged, let love, harmony
and civility be your guiding star.

Give yourself whole-heartedly to the task of serving
others regardless of friends and foes.

But the greatest message of Sufism is that when God made
man, he put into the soul his equal, his active, everlasting master-
piece. It was so great a work that it could not be otherwise than
the soul, and the soul could not be otherwise than the work of
God. "God's nature, his being, and the godhead all depend on
his work in the soul." Therefore thou shall know your God without image, without semblance and without intermediary. "I am
all but he, he all but me," cried Hallaj. "God must be very I,
I very God. This He and this I are one." God is love, and as
Creator, he can never be outside the creature.

Rumi, in the Prologue to Masnavi, laments about the banishment of man from his home and his temporary separation
from that soul which connects him with God:

Hearken to the reed-flute, how it complains,
Lamenting its banishment from its home:—

"Ever since they tore me from my osier bed,
My plaintive notes have moved men and women to tears.
I burst my breast, striving to give vent to sighs,
And to express the pangs of my yearning for my home
Is ever longing for the day he shall return.
My wailing is heard in every throng,
In concert with them that rejoice and them that weep.
"Each interprets my notes in harmony with his own feelings,

But not one fathoms the secrets of my heart.
My secrets are not alien from my plaintive notes,
Yet they are not manifest to the sensual eye and ear.
Body is not veiled from soul, neither soul from body,
Yet no man had ever seen a soul.
This plaint of the flute is fire, not mere air.
Let him who lacks this fire be accounted dead!
'Tis the fire of love that inspires the flute,[9]
'Tis the ferment of love that possesses the wine.
The flute is the confidant of all the lovers;
Yea, its strains lay bare my inmost secrets.
Who hath seen a poison and antidote like the flute?
Who hath seen a sympathetic consoler like the flute?
The flute tells the tale of love's bloodstained path,
It recounts the story of Majnun's love toils.
Arise, O Son! Burst thy bonds and be free!
How long wilt thou be captive to silver and gold?
Though thou pour the ocean into thy pitcher,
It can hold no more than one day's store.
The pitcher of the desire of the covetous never fills,
The oyster-shell fills not with pearls till it is content;
Only he whose garment is rent by the violence of love
Is wholly pure from covetousness and sin.
Hail to thee, then, O love, sweet madness!
Thou who healest all our infirmities!
Who are the physician of our pride and self conceit.

"Who art our Plato and our Galen!
Love exalts our earthly bodies to heaven,
And makes the very hills to dance with joy!
O lover, it was Love that gave life to Mount Sinai,
When 'it quaked, and Moses fell down in a swoon.'
Did my Beloved only touch me with his lips
I too, like the flute, would burst out in melody.
But he who is parted from them that speak his tongue,
Though he possessed a hundred voices, is perforce dumb.
When the rose has faded and the garden is withered,
The song of the nightingale is no longer to be heard.
The Beloved is all in all, the lover only veils Him;

---

[9] Love signifies the strong attraction that draws all creatures back to reunion with their Creator.

The Beloved is all that lives, the lover a dead thing.
When the lover feels no longer Love's quickening,
He becomes like a bird who has lost its wings. Alas!
How can I retain my senses about me,
When the Beloved shows not the light of His countenance?
Love desires that this secret should be revealed,
For if a mirror reflects not, of what use is it?
Knowest thou why thy mirror reflects not?
Because the rust has not been scoured from its face.
If it were purified from all rust and defilement,
It would reflect the shining of the Son of God.
O friends, ye have now heard this tale,
Which sets forth the very essence of my case."[10]

Al-Ghazali, referred to as the Saint Augustine of Sufism, also states that "the superiority of man consists in his being cognizant of divine attributes and actions. Therein lies his perfection; thus he may be worthy of admission to God's presence. The body serves as a vehicle for the divine soul, and the soul is the abode for knowledge which is its fundamental character as well as its ultimate object. If man wishes for true happiness, let him look upon reason as a monarch setting on the throne of his heart, imagination as its ambassador, memory as treasurer, speech as interpreter, the limbs as clerks, and the senses as spies in the realms of color, sound, smell etc."[11]

---

[10] Rumi, Masnavi, translated by E. H. Whinfield.
[11] Al-Ghazali, Ihv Al Ulum (Teheran: Majlis Publication, 1931), p. 61.

# Index